AVENUES TOWARD CHRISTIANITY
Mormonism in Comparative Church History

AVENUES TOWARD CHRISTIANITY
Mormonism in Comparative Church History

Christian Gellinek
Hans-Wilhelm Kelling

Studies of the Latter-Day Saint Religion
Academic Studies in Religion and the Social Order
Global Publications, Binghamton University
Binghamton, New York
2001

Library of Congress Cataloging-in-Publication Data

Gellinek, Christian.
[Christus in Amerika? English]
Avenues toward Christianity : Mormonism in comparative church history
/ Christian Gellinek, Hans-Wilhelm Kelling.
p. cm. -- (Academic studies in religion and the social order)
Includes bibliographical references.
ISBN 1-58684-128-9
1. Church of Jesus Christ of Latter-Day Saints--Doctrines. 2. Mormon Church--Doctrines. 3. Church of Jesus Christ of Latter-Day Saints--Relations. 4. Mormon Church--Relations. 5. Church history. I. Kelling, Hans-Wilhelm. II. Title. III. Series.
BX8635.2 .G45 2001
289.3'09--dc21

2001004125

Published and Distributed by:
Studies of the Latter-Day Saint Religion
Academic Studies in Religion and the Social Order
Global Publications, Binghamton University
LNG 99, Binghamton University
State University of New York, USA 13902-6000
Phone: (607) 777-4495 or 777-6104; Fax: (607) 777-6132
E-mail: pmorewed@binghamton.edu
http://ssips.binghamton.edu

ACADEMIC STUDIES IN RELIGION AND THE SOCIAL ORDER
Publisher: Global Publications, State University of New York at Binghamton
Address: LNG 99, SUNY-Binghamton, Binghamton, New York 13902-6000

STUDIES OF THE LATTER-DAY SAINT RELIGION

This book is dedicated to Douglas F. Tobler

Table of Contents

Foreword

This study constitutes a division of labor between two trusted colleagues. The basis of this new book is Christian Gellinek's *Christus in Amerika?* published in 1999 by the Agenda Verlag in Münster, Germany. Professor Hans-Wilhelm Kelling, Brigham Young University, Provo, Utah, offered to translate the bulk of it into English. At the same time Gellinek worked on additions in English, based on talks given June 25 - July 2, 2000 at The Thirty-Fifth Annual Meeting of the Mormon History Association in Copenhagen and Aalborg, Denmark, commemorating 150 Years of Mormonism in Continental Europe. He also included his new research about the language usage of the Mormons. On the other hand, some German sections were shortened, clarified or omitted altogether. As the book must be considered a newly enlarged and revised edition, and benefits from Kelling's deeper knowledge of the LDS Church, the credit is shared by a co-authorship of both. However, the ultimate responsibility rests with Christian Gellinek.

Gellinek's interest in Mormonism began with an invitation to be a visiting professor at the University of Utah in 1977. At that time his new colleagues Wolff A. von Schmidt and Gerhard P. Knapp invited him to publish an article in the *Festschrift für Arval L. Streadbeck zum 65. Geburtstag*, which appeared in 1981. It deals with the pertinent topic, "The Defense of the Truth of Christian Religion from 1540-1631" by the Spaniard Juan Luis Vives, the Frenchman Philippe Duplessis Mornay, the Dutchman Hugo Grotius, and the School of the German poet Martin Opitz. There Hugo Grotius's *Origin of the American Natives* (1642) is briefly mentioned. Subsequently Gellinek researched and published the first American biography of Hugo Grotius in 1983 dealing with his legal, poetical, historical, and ecclesiastical works in both Latin and Dutch. In the seventeenth century the truth of the Christian religion was a poetical topic of the so-called elegant school of jurisprudence. From 1641 to 1644 Grotius wrote a then world-famous annotated commentary on both The New and The

Old Testament of together 2777 pages. This work forms the background and planted the seed for studies of Mormonism. I also benefitted from teaching a graduate course on the "True Religion" theme in comparative Renaissance literature at UCLA in 1984.

Many colleagues gave a helping hand by discussing the subject, looking over the manuscript and, in some cases, suggesting corrections. Others kept in touch by e-mail. A work such as this one is indebted to several willing minds. I am very thankful to have benefitted from the advice of Thomas G. Alexander, Peter Crawley, Mario S. DePillis, Harold W. Draper, Eric Eliason, Dean of the College of Humanites Van Gessel, the legal historian Heinz Holzhauer, Paul Y. Hoskisson, Neal Kramer, Don LeFevre, James K. Lyon, Don Norton, Dallin Oaks, Daniel C. Peterson, John S. Robertson, Royal Skousen, Douglas F. Tobler, John W. Welch, Jedford Woodworth, and last but not least Victor H. Yngve.

I am also grateful to the interlibrary loan service of the University of South Florida in Tampa, Florida, to the fifth floor staff of the Harold B. Lee Library at Brigham Young University in Provo, Utah, and particularly to the user friendly staff members of the L. Tom Perry Americana and Mormonism Special Collections & Manuscripts Unit. The co-authors thank Matthew Hamby for making this manuscript copy ready. In Shalahudin Kafrawi our publisher provided us with a patient programmer and a gifted graphic scanner at the same time. We also benefited from James Vaughn's professional advice.

Introduction

This study intends to describe a phenomenon which today has found acceptance in American everyday culture, but remains in Germany, and in many other parts of the world, either totally unfamiliar to many people or is perceived only as a distorted stereotype. For this reason I wrote the original version for a German audience in German. Until recently such a study had not yet been published in the German language for the German reader. With this new publication I will attempt to reduce or completely eliminate grave misunderstandings in the minds of the reader. I would also like to offer new insights and provide an increased understanding of Mormonism to both German and American members of the Church of Jesus Christ of Latter-day Saints and to non-Mormons as well. The frame work of my investigation consists of universal church history.

The original unfinished manuscript in German was presented *in absentia* in the spring 1998 to faculty members of Brigham Young University in Provo, Utah. I was encouraged to complete the manuscript and invited to spend four months on the campus during the fall semester 1998 where I benefitted from the advice of several colleagues and from frank discussions with them. My research in the Harold B. Lee Library enabled me to fill in gaps and add essential details. Thus the manuscript which I had brought along from Germany, was gradually completed and received its final academically acceptable form.

Basics needed almost no amending, mostly accents had to be placed differently, an addition had to be made here or there and occasionally a more exacting detail enclosed. The progressive chapter structure took into account the interests of educated non-Mormon readers as well as members of the Church of Jesus Christ of Latter-day Saints who would like to increase their knowledge.

The final German version aims to clearly set a foundation for a comparative examination of church history, in chapters I, II and III by historical and in chapter IV by biographical investigations, in chapter V by a comparative approach. In this connection it must be pointed out that a "new approach" to writing Mormon history (*The American West*, 1969) was introduced by Moses Rishin thirty years ago and has found only gradual, if not reluctant acceptance. How much more formidable are the difficulties a non-Mormon with predominantly theoretical knowledge had to overcome in order to paint a coherent picture of Mormonism. Many insights had remained rather unclear or fuzzy, until I was able to pursue my research again in 1999 on the campus of Brigham Young University.

The German version of this book was positively reviewed by Richard D. Hacken in "BYU Studies" 39, 1, 2000, 212-214, but the Mormon guild generally did not take issue. During a third research stay at Brigham Young University in the fall 2000, the issues were further clarified, and the author was persuaded not to pursue a new book project, *Avenues toward Mormonism.* Instead he opted to join with an experienced translator and scholar, his colleague at Brigham Young University Professor Hans-Wilhelm Kelling, and invited him as coauthor to engage in a friendly but lively debate. Thus from time to time Kelling adds clarification and insight which enhances the present volume. This partnership provided an opportunity to produce a new enlarged version in English and to include scientific material presented at the Thirty-Fifth Annual Conference of the Mormon History Association in Aalborg, Denmark. Ambiguities could be changed, deliberate ambiguity ironed out and a fifth chapter added. The new title reflects the changes as well. The book now focuses on the process and intends to provide particularly the Mormon reader with more depth. Instead of the original fifth chapter, which the reviewer deemed too short, an original linguistic contribution is attempted for which I accept sole responsibility.

My methodology depends on insights which I was able to gain step by step. My partner and I want to eliminate misconceptions with this study. While working on my book, I was able to liberate myself from stereotypical prejudices which I had originally held about Mormonism. I could not have foreseen this additional result of my research. In the following chapters it will also be made clear in which sense — surely not in the sense of Arthur Schopenhauer — Mormons are right after all and to what extent certain qualifications must be maintained within the framework of this study.

My study is a representation of the phenomenon and the significance, i.e. the developmental process, of a Christian church. Gradually I want to clarify relationships which emerged and underwent adjustment during 170 years of church history. I wish to present the results of my research to the seeker of information in a manner readily understandable and readable, but at the same time in a scholarly and academically accepted fashion as well.

Professor Gellinek has graciously invited Professor Kelling to join him in preparing this book, and I (Kelling) wish to thank him for that. It has been a distinct pleasure to work and deliberate together, and from our cooperation a genuine friendship and admiration has developed which, I believe, had a salutary effect on our work.

1. General Introduction to Church-Historical Problems of Mormonism: Apocrypha and Canon

Failure by parents and grandparents (in support of parents) to provide for their children guiding principles in matters of faith, is regarded today by churches as a serious threat to family unity. But how are parents to proceed? The faith of their ancestors generally remains unknown or mysterious to children today.[1] Although ancestors have placed their genetic stamp of the divine image on their descendants, they are no longer considered to be a valid model by the average modern family. Too often do younger family members consider the convictions and the religious practices of their forebears to be old fashioned.[2] Modern family centered Mormonism is an exception. It is a flourishing religious community that was founded in 1820 by only a few families who cultivated personal interaction.

Parallel to the above problem, the books of the Bible, which until recently were regarded as obligatory and authoritative, are nowadays either severely criticized or ignored. For centuries the canon firmly held together the books of the New and the Old Testament and was accepted as the sole measure of authoritative judgement in matters of faith. But that is no longer true. Today theological interpretation replaces the obedient faith of a family. Thus many a minister has become an interpreter rather than a preacher of the Christian message for individuals who assemble for the purpose of accepting it. Christi-

---

[1]According to an EMNID survey conducted in 1997 only 17% of Germans believe in God as "a personal being". See: "Auf dem Rückzug?" *Monatshefte*, vol. 51, 379. *The Historical Atlas of Religion in America* (New York, 1962) lists similar low statistics for Americans in the period from 1790 to 1800.

[2]A Forsa-survey found that for only 40% of Germans, belief in God is important. Half of Catholics are not interested in saints. See: *Weltbild,* 12 Sep. 1997, 8-13.

anity no longer fully proclaims the joyous message of salvation but instead makes a variety of verbal offers to anonymous persons.

Of course there are movements opposing these trends. Preoccupation with the question, as to whether Christianity has remained watchful and sufficiently receptive to new ideas and whether it has been able to constantly defend and further develop its message, which is under attack, has greatly changed and splintered it during the last five generations. Thus Protestant Christianity split and developed into various religious denominations, and, to be sure, not always under its own impulse.

Rather than constantly asking new questions of the books of the Bible which have become a canon, and of the traditional meaning of their text, the possibility should be considered that there may exist a testament which was hidden for a long time. Suddenly, in the 19th century, such a record was discovered, discussed and became rather well known. This newly discovered text is the Book of Mormon.

Apocrypha is an ancient Hellenistic expression for secret books, that suddenly appear. Martin Luther translated the pertinent passage in scripture as follows: "They are books, although not equal to Holy Scripture, yet useful and good to read."[3] Before they became generally known, they were appreciated only by a circle of initiates. Surprisingly, they later claimed authoritative acceptance which, however, is still denied them by the dominant churches. Thus they are not included in the established canon. Their content is regarded as sectarian.[4]

---

[3]*Die Bibel oder die Heilige Schrift des Alten und Neuen Testaments nach der deutschen Übersetzung von D. Martin Luther's.* Privilegierte Württembergische Bibelanstalt Stuttgart, n.d. [1946], Anhang: Die Apokryphen, 1.

[4]*Der kleine Pauly. Lexikon der Antike in fünf Bänden* (Munich, 1979), vol. 1, col. 436.

Judged by historically developed guidelines, apocrypha are not canonical. Only the accepted canon is considered to be non-apocryphal, i.e. fully authentic. "False sources" have been deliberately added to "genuine sources" of the apocrypha to the New Testament. As far as apocryphal books to the Old Testament are concerned, " ... an actual continuation of the history of revelation is intended", to be sure "honestly, even if by profane hands."[5] For this reason an interest in such parallel traditions must be cultivated more in the Lutheran than in the Catholic Church. The Catholic Church accepted several apocrypha of the Old Testament but does not regard them as equally authentic as the canonical books, while the Lutherans look on them suspiciously as a possible trap of dogmatic deviations, however at times also as worth considering.

After 1825 "powerful forces originating primarily in England agitated for the complete removal of the apocrypha from Bible editions."[6] This had important consequences. From the viewpoint of the canon the apocrypha were of insignificant importance. The vacuum is filled by an apocryphal record "of honest intent" which represents an actual continuation of the Jewish and Christian History of Revelation before and after the birth of Christ: The Book of Mormon.

The original English language edition of the Book of Mormon was published in 1830 in Palmyra, New York. It consists of fifteen books, the first ten of which give an account beginning 600 years B.C. and ending one year before Christ's birth.[7] Joseph Smith, the young son of a New York farmer, testifies in the first edition of the apocryphally

---

[5]Rudolf Hofmann, "Apokryphen", in *Realencyclopaedie für protestantische Theologie und Kirche* (Leipzig, 1896), 654, also 622-670.

[6]*Realencyclopaedie,* 628. Rh. James Montague, *The Lost Apocrypha of the Old Testament*, No. 1, 1920/1936, IX. Hugh Nibley, *An Approach to the Book of Mormon,* chapter 16. Stephen E. Robinson, *Are Mormons Christians?* (Salt Lake City, 1991), 54-55.

[7]The Book of Mormon, 1 Nephi 1; Helaman 16:25.

handed down record that he "translated" the account from metal plates he had discovered.[8]

That may mean a number of things, among others, that by way of a substantial temporal detour a new incursion is made into the prophetic era of the New Testament. The Book of Mormon does not, however, claim categorically to replace canonized prophetic statements. Basically this prophetic book appeals to the receptive mood of 19th century protesting Christians. It proposes to be an "abridgment"[9] or a spiritual restoration of a handed-down record that was initially translated by the prophet Joseph Smith and thereafter edited by subsequent modern scribes.

The last five books of the Book of Mormon are somewhat different. They cover a time period from the first year A.D. to the year 421 of modern time.[10] With the annunciation of the appearance of Christ in the eleventh chapter of 3 Nephi, the prototype and the direction of the thrust of the Joseph Smith translation, prevailing up to this point, is modified. From this point on, the emphasis is placed on Christ's appearance in America and on His teachings. Thus the revelation of the New Testament is not merely changed by various infusions, but is in many ways restored, confirmed and clarified.

The 3 Nephi text is a record which pursues a different approach than the sections preceding it. The last fourth of the book is told vividly and powerfully but different from the part before. Consequently this last part of the Book of Nephi may be regarded by orthodox Christians as being heretical, and therefore I will attempt in subsequent

---

[8]This statement is qualified on the title page: "And now, if there are faults they are the mistakes of men."

[9]The 1966 German edition translates abridgment correctly as "Abkürzung", while Immo Luschin in his 1976 translation calls it "Auszug" which actually means excerpt or extract and is not exactly the same as an abridgment.

[10]The Book of Mormon, 3 Nephi to Moroni.

pages of my book to refute any claims of heresy — and I trust to be successful in this endeavor.

In the course of my investigation I must return from time to time to this inclusion in the Book of Mormon of a visit by Christ to the "American" continent. (I believe, for non-members of the LDS Church this inclusion represents one of the major difficulties in interpreting the Book.) It is apparent, although not always entirely familiar to every Christian, that the Christian faith as such has, so to speak, geographically constantly 'roamed'. However, the fact that Christ in the first century after the turn of the meridian appeared in what later became known as America, is entirely new.

Accordingly I initially intended to publish my former book version with the title "Christ immigrates to America".[11]

I will now briefly recapitulate the said migration of the Christian faith. Original Christianity initially migrated from Palestine to Egypt, Mesopotamia and Asia Minor. According to the *Acts of the Apostles* (XVI), the Apostle Paul on his extensive, not always voluntary journeys, came to Greece.[12] This disciple of Christ is later taken as a prisoner to Rome. There he interacted with Christians that had already arrived before him. As Christ's faithful apostle he was executed in Rome. Under the rule of the East-Roman Emperor Constantine, Christianity ceased to be a despised religion of outsiders and slaves. Persecution had become so rare that Constantine was able to tolerate Christianity and accord it equal rights among the other religions. Because of this

---

[11]It would be a daring hypothesis to explain the last portion of the Book of Mormon, Fourth Nephi, as representing a kind of extra-geographic intermediate realm. Richard L. Bushman is noticeably reticent to discuss this point in his *Making Space for the Mormons: Ideas of Sacred Geography in Joseph Smith's America*, 1997. The subtitle is left off in the publication deposited in the archives of the Brigham Young University Harold B. Lee Library.

[12]The Acts of the Apostles 20.

new assessment, Christianity in the year 313 received legal status through the Edict of Toleration.[13]

Around the year 600 A.D., the power of the Bishop of Rome had become so firmly established that Pope Gregory I could send missionaries to England. Before his martyrdom at the hands of the Friesians in 754, Winfried the Edeling of Exeter called Bonifatius, brought Christianity to the Thuringians and Hessians in what is today Germany. Now the question arises, can the dispersing of Christianity be regarded as a consolidation of the Christian faith outside of its original Near-Eastern heartland and outside of Greece and Rome, and can it be considered as well as gradually asserting itself in each new region; or must it be regarded as *peregrinatio fidei* [the spreading of a strange new faith] and a new religious movement that came about as a result of the migration of Christianity? While thousands of the disciples of Christ migrated to Syria, Ethiopia and other parts of the world, Jesus himself, according to the account of the New Testament — which by the way was canonized only in the course of subsequent centuries — remained throughout his mortal life in Palestine. To be sure, other gospels exist, as for example the Gospel of Thomas. But now, according to the account in the Book of Mormon, Jesus Christ is seen and heard overseas in the year 34 A.D. What are we to make of that?

After Church-Christianity had allied itself with the power of the state, it became a universal religion addressing everyone on all continents, also people in South and North America, starting in the 16th century. Now the imperative of the resurrected Christ to baptize all nations[14] so that they might receive salvation, became efficacious even to people on the American continent.

---

[13]Rodney Stark, *The Rise of Christianity* (Princeton University Press, 1996).

[14]Matthew 28:19-20; Mark 16:15-16.

In North America, English speaking New England was in the 17th century just as receptive to the spread and assimilation of Christianity as the people who had remained behind on the British Isles. After several stages, the biblical tradition had now reached the colonies and there precipitated additional dispute over the interpretation of biblical texts.

A thousand year late, the Council of Trent[15] declared the biblical text canonical. After that, the division of the New Testament into books placed in a firm sequence was unchangeable so that ironically even the Jewish Bible accepted the canonical order of the Vulgate.[16] Further additions were not considered feasible until new words of Jesus would be found or revealed.

Work on the authorized edition of the English Bible began shortly after King James I acceded to the throne in 1604 and ended in 1611. An impartially organized committee of the finest divinity scholars of the realm was named and, divided into six "companies", completed the translation work in two years and nine months. As their basis served the Tyndale-Bible and other acceptable translations, which already existed in English translations. A conference consisting of members from the high and the low church was summoned to mediate opposing positions. The Bible translation was carefully revised and presented to the king as the King James Version. This version was also the standard in North America from 1830 to 1881.[17]

The qualification of the Mormons with respect to the correct Bible translation becomes therefore understandable. In the eighth Article of Faith the qualification reads: "We believe the Bible to be the Word of

[15]Trent, a city in Northern Italy, at that time belonged to the Holy Roman Empire of the German Nation.

[16]H. Hunger et al., ed., *Die Textüberlieferung der antiken Literatur und der Bibel* (Dtv, 1989) 2nd ed., 152ff., 190ff and 425.

[17]David Daiches, *The King James Version of the English Bible* (Archeon Books, 1968).

God as far as it is translated correctly." However, Joseph Smith, his scribe Oliver Cowdery and the printer Grandin accepted the antiquated and stylized Bible English oft the 17th century[18] and while thus making the writing and printing of the text more difficult[19] made it on the other hand more acceptable to the reader at that time. Even though the American Bible reader of the 18th and early 19th century accepted many revolutionary ideas, he nevertheless held on firmly to the values and standards of the English language. It required inordinate concentration on the part of Joseph Smith when dictating to his various scribes an apocryphically handed-down history of revelation, a text of considerable volume: the Book of Mormon.

It was inevitable during the more than 170 year old church history of Mormonism that the textual concordance to the revised King James Version – as also to Bible versions in any other language – had to be reexamined, especially since 1 Nephi 13:23 acknowledges the present text of the Bible to be "of great worth unto the Gentiles", i.e. to the so-called "non-Jews." That had to be of special importance if the posthumous writings (as for example *The Pearl of Great Price*) of the Prophet Joseph Smith could not be considered equal to the degree of inspiration apparent in the Book of Mormon. The result was a gradation problem concerning Mormon texts. In the so-called *Pearl of Great Price* [20] not all posthumous texts are equal to the revelatory tradition of the Book of Mormon. A ranking and weighing of the Old

---

[18]In older German editions, as well as in translations of the Book of Mormon into other living languages, the many (almost 2000) "lo and behold" and "it came to pass" were omitted. The omission was indicated by square brackets. Some Mormon scholars believe that these figures of speech are genuine elements of ancient texts.

[19]For example because of the treatment of nouns which in the English of 1830 were no longer capitalized.

[20]The *Pearl of Great Price* was published 1852 in Illinois and is a posthumous collection containing a "Book of Moses". It has attained almost canonical rank, but the "Book of Abraham" also contained in the collection, is for technical reasons not to be regarded fully authentic. See commentary by Donna Hill, *Joseph Smith: The First Mormon* (New York, 1979), 193ff. and 3.2 below.

Testament, the New Testament, the Book of Mormon, the Pearl of Great Price, and the Doctrine and Covenants appears in order, is however difficult to do. Inasmuch as they all contain and convey God's word, a ranking is out of the question. Instead another way was found out of this dilemma.

The leadership of the Church authorized the preparation of a special King James Version for members of the church which not only points out related and parallel verses between the Book of Mormon and the Bible, but also parallel texts of Bible verses to the Book of Mormon including commentaries. The position of modern Mormons clearly indicates that the Book of Mormon supplements the two Testaments; yet it does not replace them. The most recent glosses provided on the bottom of each page of the Mormon King James Version, published for the first time in 1979, are not based on newly discovered manuscripts, but are commentaries, which are to enlighten either record in both directions.[21]

Accordingly the newest version of the Book of Mormon published in German, for example, has the subtitle: "Ein weiterer Zeuge [sic] für Jesus Christus."[22] [Another Witness for Jesus Christ.] This new subtitle was also added to the English and other translated editions. It is absent in the 1966 edition. Something had changed in the dogmatic thinking of Mormonism.

Concerning the understanding of dogma, it seems that Mormonism does not merely primarily emphasize the irrefutable definition of the

---

[21]THE HOLY BIBLE ... Authorized King James Version (Salt Lake City, 1995).

[22]Horst Reller in his *Handbuch religiöser Gemeinschaften*, 4th ed., (Gütersloh, 1993), in Section 3, Sekten, argues on pp. 390-406 "any relation to Christianity is hardly recognizable." An article published by the Seminary for Practical Theology of the University of Hamburg with the title "Kirche Jesu Christi der Heiligen der Letzten Tage" in *Lexikon der Hamburger Religionsgemeinschaften* (Dölling und Galitz Verlag, 1994) is much more insightful.

faith, but rather a changing framework of adapting new definitions as an aid for comprehension. Thus, when the phrase "an additional witness for Christ" was added to the title of the Book of Mormon, it denotes on the one hand that the believing community has grown in understanding and on the other hand that the Book of Mormon does not proclaim superiority to the Christian message of the New Testament. To use a system-analytical expression, the new edition of the Book of Mormon and the newest King James Version are concerned with an approximate rectification of "untenable insecurities", while at the same time desiring to harmonize contradictions.[23] This is delivered by what may be called a spiritual conciliation between apocrypha and canon and a harmonization of the two Testaments.[24] Despite the evident careful commitment to these matters, neither Mormonism nor any other modern religious community can totally do away with the uncertainties of the salvation-seeker who hopes to find certainty in sacred texts. The message itself can not completely erase lingering doubt by means of authoritative statements. Therefore, the canon is not a hermetically closed but rather a very much alive message. In its present form the Book of Mormon knocks on the gate of the canon.

1.1 Orientation: Getting the German Reader Attuned

In the meantime it may have become more obvious to the reader, why an English Bible text composed by a committee, a text that absolutely excludes apocrypha, poses the following question: Is this text totally correct and is the translation finite? The question, which denomination interprets a genuine text correctly, occupied the young Joseph Smith's thinking even before he was fifteen years old. On account of the different opinions held by the various denominations, he and his

---

[23]Niklas Luhmann, "Religionsdogmatik und gesellschaftliche Evolution" ed. K.W. Dahm et alii, *Religion – System – und Sozialisation* (Darmstadt, 1972), 15-132.

[24]Most important in this process is the incorporation of the New Testament subject: The appearance of Christ after his resurrection (34 A.D.) overseas (America).

family became confused. Which revival theology of which denomination was to serve the youth as a guideline, the one proclaimed by the Congregationalists, the Presbyterians, the Methodists or the Baptists? Instead of confusing this yet relatively unschooled young mind with long-winded, theological interpretations[25] – he was a farm boy lacking a systematic education – it would have been preferable for him to be taught by convincing prophecy. This method was fairly popular during the early part of the 19th century in both America and England. To be sure, prophecies of the past and of the future would have to be differentiated. According to the Bible, a prophecy can only be regarded as genuine if it does not originate "from one's own experience".[26] The young doubter found the records of the Book of Mormon because his prayers had been answered. He followed the path of clarification by receiving visitations from God, Jesus Christ and other heavenly messengers which led to prophecy. The thoughtful patience with which Joseph Smith accomplished his mission is astounding. He had to wait for four years before he was permitted to lift the plates from the Hill Cumorah in New York State and before he began the challenging and difficult task of translating the hieroglyphics inscribed upon the plates.[27]

It may suffice at this point to mention that many evangelical revival preachers during the early 19th century believed that church activities at that time had deteriorated, were bigoted and totally lacking spirituality. Revival sermons concentrating on expounding God's power in novel and often unexpected ways, were popular in pre-industrialized

---

[25]Think of the nonconformist theology of the English writer and teacher John Pye Smith (no relation) (1774-1851) who in 1818-21 had published *The Scripture Testimony to the Messiah*, a treatise that extensively expounds Christ as a godman.

[26]2 Peter 1:20-21. The venerable handed-down church saying must be noted: "deus [testis] qui nec falli nec fallere potest", which is to say, no one, especially not a witness, can deceive out of ignorance. Joseph Smith's parents and some of his brothers and sisters thought so as well about his religious vision of 1820. Cf. L. J. Arrington, Davis Bitton, *The Mormon Experience* (Vintage Press, 1980), 3.

[27]Refer to 3.1 for a detailed account of the translation work.

England. Well- trained Mormon missionaries benefitted from this fact and were able to convert listeners by preaching faith, baptism and confession. In the "missionary center" of America, LDS ministers were called and ordained but not appointed to the priesthood and rendered assistance and leadership without pay. The LDS Church does not have a professional, paid ministry. LDS men holding the priesthood perform missions and the work of the ministry in an honorary capacity just like the early Christians did.

American Mormon missionaries paying their own way while proselyting in England and Sweden proclaimed their message powerfully and with great enthusiasm. They were convinced that their new American homeland possessed a newly revealed religious history that was just as ancient as that of sorely afflicted Europe. Divinely called, missionaries often facing resistance and disparagement proclaimed their concrete gospel message: "We believe it just to preach the gospel to the nations of the earth, and warn the righteous to save themselves from the corruption of the world."[28] Missionaries preached the restored gospel first in Europe, but today they are active in almost all nations of the world.

One must ask why special "documents" were necessary to commence the work of conversion. In addition to the testimony and enthusiasm of the missionaries, this rational aspect was important to the skeptics at that time who were disillusioned with their own churches but receptive to the new gospel. The converts were mainly Englishmen who came to America after their conversion and Americans who had settled the Western border regions.

Restored Christianity could be preached most enthusiastically both at home and abroad because Christ had been seen and heard in Amer-

---

[28]Doctrine and Covenants, Section 134:12. This section was adopted by unanimous vote at a general assembly of the Church in Kirtland, Ohio on August 17, 1835.

ica shortly after his resurrection. Counter-Puritans, who were called by the nickname "Mormons", were able to deepen and liberate religious life primarily among the lower classes of England by preaching a new gospel. They were very successful, as we shall see.

1.2 The Book of Mormon and its Dissemination in Germany

Figure 1: The first Book of Mormon in German, 1852.

Written in biblical style, the Book of Mormon is an account of two pre-Columbian people (one originating in Babel the other in Jerusalem). According to the book's account, descendants of the ten lost tribes of Israel[29] landed in two consecutive immigration waves in Central America. They fought several battles in the course of their history. The final battle took place in 385 A.D. near a hill[30] which is located in America. (By the way, at about this time Augustine becomes Bishop of Hippo in North Africa.) Mormon, the last leader of his people, gathered and abridged the sacred records before this final battle, then, before he died, turned them over to his son Moroni who completed the records and then hid them from his enemies in the Hill Cumorah. The records were engraved on gold-like metal plates and preserved for posterity. Some American Indian tribes are believed to be descendants of Israelites.[31] The book is named after the ancient prophet-leader Mormon. I will discuss the book in more detail in the historical section 3.1 below.

I personally held in my hand and examined the 1830 leather-bound original edition in duodecimo-format. In that edition Joseph Smith, Jr. is listed as author and owner of the rights to the book.[32]

Joseph Smith started to dictate the record in December 1827. The work had to be interrupted for several longer periods and must have

---

[29]Actually only the second group claim to be descendants of Joseph (1Nephi 5:14). The first group were descendants of Noah who left Babel before the dispersion of Israel.

[30]Early scholars believed that this hill was the Hill Cumorah which is located in today's State of New York. More recent scholars think it was in Mexico. Consult John L. Sorenson, *An Ancient American Setting for the Book of Mormon* (Salt Lake City, 1985).

[31]Hugh Nibley, *An Approach to the Book of Mormon,* 3rd ed. (Salt Lake City, 1988), annotation 6 and Sorenson annotation 30.

[32]According to Professor Royal Skousen the proprietorship later became unimportant and was dropped in the second edition of 1837. Joseph Smith acquired the copyright in the office of the Northern section of New York State on June 11, 1830.

lasted a few months. It was primarily done in Harmony, Pennsylvania.[33] The Prophet neither prepared the chapter headings nor did he correct the galley proofs himself. The text was not yet set in columns.[34] The printing of the first edition of 5000 copies had been financed by the well-to-do farmer Martin Harris. Each volume was to be sold for $1.25.[35] During the next 50 years the thousands of English converts desired a more lucid text with cross references. Thus in 1879 the intellectual apostle and mathematician Orson Pratt (1811-1881) added the divisions into chapter and verse which is still used in modern editions. As an experienced foreign missionary, Hyde aided in systematizing the Mormon religion.

The lawyer, theologian and preacher Orson Spencer (1802-1855) was, as far as we know, the first missionary in Prussia (1850), but he was not able to establish a branch of the church (a parish).[36] Even before the first two converts were baptized on September 1851 in the Elbe-River, the missionary apostle Orson Hyde (1805-1878) was prevented in Bavaria from preaching the message of the Book of Mormon. In 1841-1842 he went on a special mission to Palestine.[37] Already in 1853 the first so-called "Sendlinge" (foreign envoys) were

---

[33]Bushman, 107-113. John W. Welch, ed. *Reexploring the Book of Mormon*. Welch writes that the work was completed in less than three months.

[34]Printer and proofreader added punctuation. I believe that the many included "lo and behold" represent breathing spaces of the dictating Joseph Smith. Does it have its origin in ancient Hebrew?

[35]Forty years later this edition had become so rare that it was sold in antiquarian bookstores for $ 10.00. Consult K. R. Hagenbach, *Kirchengeschichte von der älteren Zeit bis zum 19. Jahrhundert* (Leipzig, 1872), vol. 7, pt. 2, 539.

[36]The first German edition of the Book of Mormon was published in 1852 by the American George Parker Dykes. (See picture of the title page on p. 18.) The first German branch of the Church was founded with 12 members in 1852 in Hamburg.

[37]He consecrated Palestine for the return of the Jews. For decades he served the Church as a member of the Council of the Twelve Apostles and became famous as lawyer and politician in the Territory of Utah.

expelled from Berlin and Hamburg. Some converts succeeded in circumventing the German bureaucracy by emigrating to America.[38]

After a brief period of constitutional reform, religious freedom was granted in 1849 in Copenhagen, Denmark. Accordingly, Brigham Young decided on Danish as the first foreign language translation for the Book of Mormon. Edited by Elder Peter O. Hansen (1818-1895)[39] and a Mlle Mathiesen it appeared as *Mormons Bog* in 1851 in Copenhagen. Elder George Parker Dykes (1814-1888) had learned some German and also some Danish in Wisconsin. He accompanied Apostle Erastus Snow as a traveling missionary in Denmark. Few Americans realize that in the 19th century, Denmark stretched south all the way to Altona which today is suburb of Hamburg. Until 1849, to hide from watchful Danish authorities, both Danish and German members of the Church met secretly in Hamburg. In 1850 the Royal Danish Army defeated the forces of Schleswig-Holstein at the Battle of Idstedt, and German church members hid from German police in Danish Altona between 1849 and 1864. After Prussian armies had defeated the Danes, Schleswig-Holstein in 1866 became part of Prussia. In the interim period the Book of Mormon had been distributed between Copenhagen in the north and Hamburg in the south.

In October 1851 Elder Dykes and John Taylor who later became the second president of the Church, began their translation in earnest. Dykes was ably assisted by Sarah Jensen from Schleswig and by Georg Viet, a German teacher in France. John Taylor supervised the transla-

---

[38]Joseph Kardinal Hergenroether, *Handbuch der Allgemeinen Kirchengeschichte* (Freiburg, 1925), vol. IV, 485ff. In 1850 the Mormon journal "Zions Panier" was published for a while. Beginning in 1869 the monthly publication "Der Stern" appeared with periodic interruptions.

[39]His achievement as a translator of the Book of Mormon into "Mormons Bog" is commemorated on his gravestone in Manti, Utah. Richard C. Poulsen, *The Pure Experience of Order* (Albuquerque, 1982), 81.

tion into French. After Danish, Italian and Welsh[40] German was the fourth and French the fifth foreign language translation. After a brief visit to Utah, Dykes returned to Hamburg and had the F. H. Nestler & Melle Press publish a bi-lingual translation:[41] "Das Buch Mormon — Ein Bericht. Le Livre de Mormon — Histoire Sacrée Des Peuples Aborigènes de L'Amérique.

The French title of this two-in-one edition is much more elaborate, but both subtitles are interesting. The French ***impressum*** on the back cover reads: "Paris Imprimerie de Marc Ducloux et Compagnie en vente: L'étoile de Déseret." On the front cover of the German version, an angel is depicted blowing a trumpet, holding it in his left hand and clutching under his right arm an "Evangelium", the Book of Mormon. The two editors state: "We took the liberty of setting the German text upon the even side, so that the French edition of this work may make use of the uneven (left) side, and both running texts face each other whenever they appear bound in one volume."[42] Several dozen bi-lingual copies were distributed in Berne and used by the Swiss mission as were an unknown number in Hamburg and Paris. The German-French Book of Mormon appeared in Paris and Hamburg at the same

---

[40]Gilbert W. Scharffs, *Mormonism in Germany. A History of the Church of Jesus Christ of Latter-day Saints in Germany between 1840 and 1970* (Salt Lake City, 1970), 7.

[41]The note by the editor Hyrum W. Valentine in the 1928 edition of *Das Buch Mormon* that this edition appeared in Berne, Switzerland, is incorrect. It was simply distributed in Berne as well. Also therefore, Immo Luschin's statement that the first edition "appeared" in Hamburg is incomplete. The German-French Book of Mormon appeared in both Paris and Hamburg and was subsequently distributed in the missions of France, Germany and Switzerland. The French and German versions had been double-checked by expert teachers in Boulogne and Hamburg respectively resulting in "alterations". Consult Samuel W. Taylor, *The John Taylor Papers*, vol. 1, 1836-1877, 168ff. and footnote 6.

[42]Translation is mine. I am able to report these details thanks to the courtesy of the staff of the Western Americana Room in the Harold B. Lee Library of Brigham Young University.

time and was subsequently distributed as a kind of "Euroland-edition" in the missions of France, Germany and Switzerland.

In August 1852 the first dozen and a half German speaking Mormon emigrants left Hamburg for Utah. The first president of the Hamburg Mission (1852-1854) was the Pennsylvania-Dutch Daniel Ca(i)rn who had to seek asylum in Altona after a brief imprisonment in Hamburg. At that time 128 members of the Church lived in Hamburg and surrounding areas, and in 1851 a branch was established in Flensburg. Until 1861 all German-speaking countries were included in one administrative missionary unit.[43]

Considering this brief background information, some (perhaps draft-avoiding[44]) "Danish" immigrants coming to Utah between 1852 and 1867 and again between 1919 and 1921, although Danish subjects, may actually have been German-speaking members from Schleswig-Holstein. In three of the six linguistic districts of Schleswig both German and Danish was spoken.[45] Accordingly we might revise slightly upward Alder's and Scharffs' figure of 15,000 German-speaking Saints[46] settling in Utah between 1850 and 1958.[47]

The first factual but hostile appraisal of Mormonism's dissemination into Germany was written by Theodor Olshausen, a "Citizen of Saint Louis, Missouri" who was born in 1802 in Glückstadt and died in

---

[43]Douglas D. Alder, "The German-Speaking Immigration to Utah 1850-1950," M.A. thesis, University of Utah, 1959, an excellent treatise not yet outdated.

[44]Bruce Van Orden, *Building Zion: The Latter-Day Saints in Europe* (Salt Lake City, 1996), 102. Or did they simply disobey military orders after 1863?

[45]Biernatzki's *Sprachkarte* of 1849 adapted by William Carr, *Schleswig-Holstein 1815-48: A Study in National Conflict* (Manchester, 1963), 322.

[46]The data and the bilingual antagonism (Sprachkampf) between Danish and German are overlooked by Bruce Van Orden.

[47]In his presidential address, Eric Pedersen made the point that most (Mormon?) immigrants from Denmark hailed from Danish cities. Until 1918 German was the predominant language in the cities of Abenraa, Haderslev and Tønder.

1869 in Hamburg. His *Geschichte der Mormonen oder Jüngsten-Tages-Heiligen in Nordamerika* was published by the prestigious theology publishing house Vandenhoeck and Ruprecht in 1856. Ironically 140 years later the manuscript of my recent book *Christus in Amerika* was rejected by the present publisher-owner Frau Dr. Ruprecht on the grounds that it was not anti-Mormon. In my book I maintain that Olshausen's anti-Mormon attitude may not be entirely explained from his knowledge of the revolutionary upheaval of the people of Schleswig-Holstein, nor from his lucid style, but rather from his first-hand observations written down in St. Louis. Only a short while ago I discovered that Olshausen had been a renowned attorney in Kiel and a member of the revolutionary von Reventlow cabinet of 1848 which, of course, was never recognized by the Danish King. After Olshausen had resigned from the cabinet he was, in due time, driven out of the country by the Danish and Hamburg police as a dangerous "zealot for the constitution" and liberal democrat. He emigrated to St. Louis, and from 1851 to 1865 (except for a short interval in Iowa) stayed with his brother, a printer. As the successful author of *Die Vereinigten Staaten von Nordamerika* (vol I, *The Mississippi Valley*, vol II, *Missouri and Iowa)*[48] he sent his manuscript to Göttingen. He was indeed a formidable adversary of the Mormons. No wonder that his book on Mormonism became influential in Germany and stayed so for a long time, in fact his early conversion statistics are still quoted by both anti-Mormon and Mormon writers.

After this brief interlude we will return to the publication history of the Book of Mormon. Friedrich W. Schönfeld incorporated Pratt's editorial additions in the new German edition. In the 1920 English edition, precisely checked footnotes, a pronunciation list of names

---

[48]Published in Kiel 1853-1854. The *Allgemeine Deutsche Biographie*, vol. 24, 1887 (reprinted by Duncker & Humblot, Berlin 1970), devoted nine pages to the attorney, politician and writer. See "Olshausen", 330-338. He came from a prominent family which is still producing scholars today. He was never married.

and a subject index was included. These helpful additions then also appeared in Jean Wunderlich's 1924 thoroughly reworked (it took him four years) edition of the German text. This edition was again checked by Max Zimmer in 1950 and was printed until 1966.

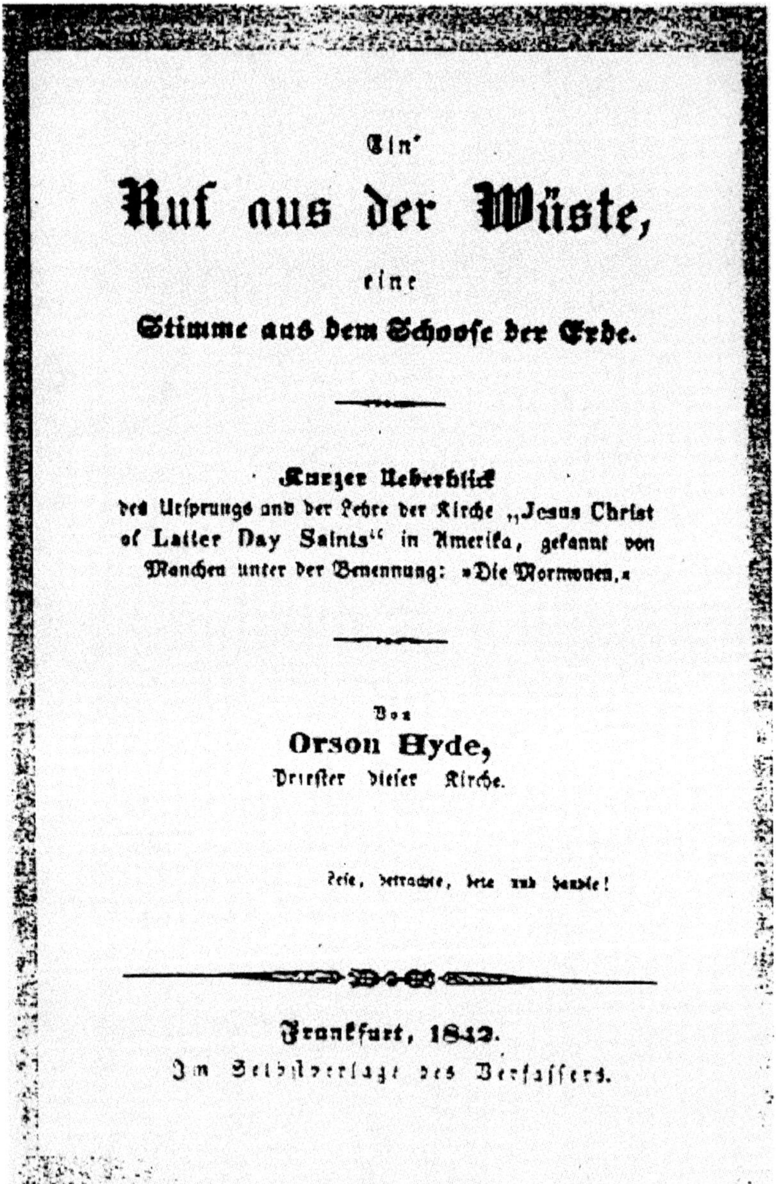

Ein

Ruf aus der Wüste,

eine

Stimme aus dem Schoose der Erde.

Kurzer Ueberblick
des Ursprungs und der Lehre der Kirche „Jesus Christ of Latter Day Saints" in Amerika, gekannt von Manchen unter der Benennung: »Die Mormonen.«

Von
Orson Hyde,
Priester dieser Kirche.

Lese, betrachte, bete und handle!

Frankfurt, 1842.
Im Selbstverlage des Verfassers.

Figure 2: "A Voice Speaking from the Desert" in German.

The most recent edition was once again reworked and "aus dem Grundtext übersetzt" (translated from the original text) by Immo Luschin between 1974 and 1979.[49] Until 1900 the Book of Mormon was only moderately received in Germany since the Church of Jesus Christ of Latter-day Saints had until then only 35 branches with about 1200 members.[50] This number is, however, much more impressive if one takes into consideration the many thousands who emigrated to Salt Lake City and the surrounding Western area.[51]

1.3 The Circulation of Supportive Publications in Germany

The careful reader of the Book of Mormon will soon become aware that besides some of the basic content, the outlines of major themes are executed in chiasm,[52] structurally complex and intertwined. Accordingly, the reader is likely to receive the impression that the message of Joseph Smith is not primarily the result of his rational thought but rather of his prophetic gift. His "translated" revelation is to cause the reader to reflect, ponder and to offer him something important to believe. Perhaps one can better appreciate the prophetic calling of the twenty-four year old Joseph Smith if one recalls that, according to John Welch, he dictated this major work within three months. In comparing later non-prophetic writings of the apostles in

---

[49]Luschin also translated "from the original" the "Doctrine and Covenants" as "Lehre und Bündnisse". The first English edition had been published in 1835. The so-called Triple Combination which in addition to the Book of Mormon and the Doctrine and Covenants included the "Pearl of Great Price" (the latter published after Joseph Smith's death in 1852 in Illinois and England) was also newly translated in revised form by Immo Luschin in 1978 and in 1985 and was again in 1995 published in Germany.

[50]*Handbuch religiöser Gemeinschaften*, 393. The numbers can not be exactly verified.

[51]According to Douglas D. Alder, "The German Immigration to Utah 1850-1950", 15,000 German speakers came to Utah.

[52]John W. Welch, "Chiasm in the Book of Mormon," *BYU Studies*, 10 (1969). "Chiasm in Alma 36," *FARMS*, 1989. In German: "Der Chiasmus im Buch Mormon" (München, 1970).

support of the prophet, and in also comparing some of Joseph Smith's own secondary writings of the eighteen-thirties and forties, differences in character and style become apparent.

Especially effective in the spreading of Mormonism in Germany was a book by Orson Pratt's older brother Parley P. (1807-1857). Both brothers were for a long time members of the Church's Council of the Twelve Apostles. "Parley", as he is generally fondly referred to, possessed not only the poetic gift of the Pratts, but his writing talent is combined with considerable editorial abilities. His most important publication is the *Stimme der Warnung* which had originally appeared in English in 1838 as *The Voice of Warning*. It was competently translated into German by Daniel Carn and printed in several editions.[53] Pratt's *Voice of Warning* is a didactic missionary tool written to reach and teach all nations in their native language, including the Germans. It is an invitation to embrace the true faith and accept the true teachings of the Church of Jesus Christ of Latter-day Saints.[54]

The Restoration of the Church, Parley maintains, is a fulfillment of prophecy. Other prophecies pertaining to future events will be fulfilled in due time. In the third chapter of his book, Pratt discusses the Kingdom of God, in the fourth the Book of Mormon, in the fifth the resurrection of the "Saints" and the restoration of those teachings

---

[53] I own the 4th edition, published by H. Dusedann, Berlin 1901. Carn was a Pennsylvanian of German descent. In 1852-53 he was the first mission president in Hamburg and Schleswig-Holstein which was Danish at that time.

[54] The popular American abbreviation for Latter-day Saints is LDS. "Latter days" refers to the church-historical concept that we now live in the end of time, in the final days before the return of the Savior. Faithful Mormons believe that the final days began with the restoration of the Church in 1830. For terminology compare Anton J. Binterim, *Die vorzüglichen Denkwürdigkeiten der Christ-Katholischen Kirche: aus den ersten, mittleren und letzten Zeiten* (Mainz, 1841). In the New Testament, saints are all those who by baptism entered into the Christian covenant (Acts 9:13,32,41). The Apostles Paul and Peter address their epistles to the saints (Rom. 1:7; 1 Cor. 1:2; Phil 1:1; 1 Pet. 1:14-15).

of Christ that had been lost, in the sixth revelation, and, in the most important seventh chapter the differences between the teachings of Jesus Christ and the departures from religious truth evident in the 19th century. In this framework the teachings of the LDS Church are proclaimed to be a restoration of the original teachings of Jesus Christ.

Since Mormonism is not always immediately comprehended by the average non-Mormon, Pratt's discourses function as practical instruction in the teachings of the LDS Church, especially since his style is very clear and vivid. He did not want "the spirit to get lost in ignorance and doubt". Missionary work probably was difficult in Germany especially in the northwest. Germans were not accustomed to missionaries preaching in the open air, as were Americans attending revival meetings. Besides, most German Christians believed that the heavens had been closed to revelation from God for centuries, that revelations, to be sure, had been written down in antiquity, and that they had most likely been translated correctly as the books of the Bible. Honest seekers of truth had not been offered on the open market such huge chunks as "the stone that was cut out of the mountain of revelation without hands."[55] The appeal to think for oneself and to make one's own decisions was foreign to Germans in the middle of the 19th century and quite suspect to the police.[56] The prophecy of Daniel would not have been considered immediately useful by a peaceful citizen of the era, especially if he would not have understood what was supposed to come of it.

As a Mormon missionary, Parley Pratt is most of all concerned with foreknowledge of things to come (like the prophet Daniel was) as if they had been pre-entered on a calendar. A solar eclipse might be predicted to occur on a certain date, since the human intellect was

---

[55]Daniel 2:45.

[56]At the time the so-called *Biedermeier* attitude was prevalent in Germany. The average German had closed his mind to outside influences in politics and religion and concentrated on family life and "tending his garden".

capable of predetermining the course of the sun. But the calendar entry of the predicted constellation would not note if the short period of darkness or the renewed occurrence of light determines spiritual knowledge and fulfills it. Pratt is concerned with the power of pre-knowing for the sake of salvation. As a comparison Pratt, at this point, interprets Daniel's well-known vision of the four worldly kingdoms,[57] and then discusses central prophecies of the New Testament and their fulfillment. He asserts that the prophecies concerning the end of time and the last days had not yet been fulfilled. Here he feels obliged to correct teachings falsely believed in the 19th century, but accepted by Protestant denominations, by opposing them with restored prophetic insights of Mormonism.[58]

Possible bottlenecks of the non-restored beliefs of other Protestant Christians appear to Pratt to result from the fixed canon committed to writing, i.e. from interpretations of biblical texts made by church officials, interpretations that had been accepted for a very long time. In contrast, Pratt and his fellow missionaries intend to spread the good news through the spoken word and by "speaking in other tongues", analogous to the miracle of Pentecost. In this manner, a missionary messenger hopes to become the mouthpiece of a higher spiritual insight which is transmitted to the investigator. In this sense the newly discovered knowledge of revelation can be considered to oppose the sterilized spirit of the enlightenment. An angel again appears in these latter days in order to renew the teachings of Christ. There is no need for a missionary to have studied theology to proclaim this good news. He resurrects the lost original Christian message. He does not proclaim carefully researched theological book learning but rather relies on inspiration received through the Holy Ghost, as was the case with Christ's apostles.

---

[57]See Christian Gellinek, "Daniel's Vision of Four Beasts," *Germanic Review*, 1966, 5-26.

[58]*Voice of Warning*, 1846 ed., 122-131.

After the former school teacher Orson Hyde had returned from the Holy Land and after he had taken private instruction in German, he wrote his own German booklet in Regensburg in 1851. He relied in part on Pratt's *Voice of Warning*, but much of the publication was original because – in contrast to Pratt – he himself had been involved in the translation. In 1840 in Nauvoo, anticipating his calling, he had already worked on the English version of the booklet which appeared in Germany under the title *Ein Ruf aus der Wüste*[59], *A Voice from the Desert.*

Like his paragon Joseph Smith who was not formally trained in English, the Apostle Hyde, proselyting in Bavaria, neither had little formal training in German stylistics. Nevertheless, Hyde writes in a popular style which even today impresses the modern reader positively with its folksy warmth. It was not difficult to translate the booklet into English.[60] Hyde gives the impression to his readers that the prophet looked through the looking glass of understanding. Hyde's version of Joseph Smith's divine calling — of which Hyde was of course convinced — is the first foreign language account of Joseph Smith's prophetic commission. Despite some grammatical mistakes — Hyde admitted to these — it is beautifully written. One can readily imagine how the first translated "Fisherman Greek" of the early apostles must have sounded to the educated class in the late first and early second century, before it was gradually smoothed out and corrected.

---

[59]*Ein Ruf aus der Wüste — eine Stimme aus dem Schoose [sic] der Erde.* (Frankfurt am Main, 1842). Cited from Dean C. Jessee, *The Papers of Joseph Smith*, Vol. I, 1989, 402-426. The picture of Hyde's title page, found on p. 26 above, is taken from Alder's MA thesis.

[60]Prof. emeritus Marvin H. Folsom translated the work into English, *Papers*, 404.

It seems obvious to me that with the simile "a voice from the desert", Hyde reminds the reader of Isaiah's "a voice from the dust".[61] In view of his sojourn in Palestine he may also point to the biblical desert of John the Baptist and by extension to the godforsaken world of Ohio and Illinois in 1840 and 1841. By combining "voice from the desert" with "voice from the womb of the earth", Hyde obviously calls attention to the long buried, hidden "sacred scriptures ... of the House of Israel" which "are to be given to other tribes scattered under the expanse of heaven".[62] Hyde accepts Pratt's characterization of the symbols engraved on the plates as "hieroglyphics", which only a few specialists could decipher and understand. He also mentions the "crystal stones" that were found along with the plates, and describes them as "having the circumference of an English crown [coin], only somewhat thicker". These stones enabled Joseph Smith to translate and dictate the text "written in letters of light" before it was returned to the heavenly messenger for safe keeping.

While pragmatic Mormonism gradually solidified and developed a progressive theology of its own, German theologians from afar acquired their own distorted picture of the church's doctrines and teachings. For decades they firmly published rejections, often with insulting rancor. They depicted Joseph Smith as a "tramp shirking work" suffering from "epileptic fits". Encyclopedic summaries under the entry "Mormons" were in the main monographs written by so-called experts who, with the exception of one Swiss writer, never set foot on Utah soil. Their hostile entries were regularly passed on, usually word for word. We might forget about these as far as their content is concerned, but will list the authors for the sake of completeness.[63] The theologian J. R. van Pelt summarizes these

---

[61]Isaiah 29. In the interpretation of Mormons "the voice from the dust" are the plates of the Book of Mormon which lay buried "in the dust" for 1200 years.

[62]This refers to non-Israelite tribes, among them the Germans.

[63]M. Busch, 1869; R. von Schlaginweit, 1874; A. Hase, 1886; D.T. Fernhagel, 1889; W. Fotsch, 1890-91.

statements in a longer article.[64] In this article all the well-known derisive attacks *ad hominem* about the church founder Joseph Smith are repeated *ad nauseam*.

1.4 The Assessment of Mormonism by German Theological Writers in the Early 20th Century

Until the turn of the century, academic broadsides were levied against solidifying Mormonism and the Church of Jesus Christ of Latter-day Saints by authors who had practically no factual knowledge of language and the area where the Mormons lived. A notable exception is the renowned Berlin Professor for Ancient History Eduard Meyer (1855-1930) who proceeded to investigate much more thoroughly. From 1908 to 1909 he traveled in the United States, spending time in Boston at Harvard University, in Madison at the University of Wisconsin and in Utah. He summarizes his basic insights about the Mormons thus: "Das Mormonentum ist nicht etwa eine Sekte, sondern eine neue Offenbarungsreligion." ("Mormonism is by no means a sect, but a new religion based on revelation.")[65] In his overall assessment Meyer does, however, commit a serious error of interpretation. In his comparison he describes Christianity as the creation of an entire generation as well as of numerous individual personalities which formed and changed it. He then contrasts Mormonism with Islam and points out that both religious movements were founded by a single prophet. His comparison is not convincing.

In the fifty years after Joseph Smith's martyrdom, and thus in plenty of time before Meyer came to the United States, Mormon beliefs had evolved and modified, as for example the concept of Adam and of

---

[64]"Mormonism" in *Realencyclopädie für protestantische Theologie und Kirche*. Albert Hauck, editor, 3rd ed., vol. 13 (Leipzig, 1903), 465-477.

[65]Eduard Meyer, *Ursprung und Geschichte der Mormonen*. Mit Exkursen über die Anfänge des Islams und des Christentums (Halle, 1912). Reprinted in the Georg Olms Verlag (Hildesheim/New York, 1970). In 1919 Meyer was appointed President of the Humboldt University in Berlin.

original sin. The burden of original sin had weighed heavily on mankind but was now lightened and lifted. The practical organization of the two branches of the priesthood, the Aaronic and the Melchizedek, had become well established. When the German professor made his observations in Utah, and later wrote his manuscript on the campus of Harvard, already the sixth prophet presided over the Church. Missionary work had been very successful. Most importantly, revelation had not and does not cease, but continues in the course of LDS church history. One might make the picturesque, somewhat daring statement: step by step the path to the light had been freed from the shadows. Spiritual life developed continuously. Meyer should have noticed the parallel evolution between the ecclesiastical and the new intellectual and worldly life in the recently founded State of Utah, for the distance between state and church had widened, and the effect on life in the Church and on its various parishes had become more obvious. To his credit, Meyer did however state that the stereotypical accusations which had been leveled by outsiders against the Mormons "were morally not justified".[66] It was impossible to simply misunderstand and misrepresent the repercussions and their echo on the development of the new State of Utah in regard to the increasingly stabilizing reality of Mormonism. His traditional Lutheran background caused the German professor nevertheless to reject the theology of the LDS Church. Placing Mormonism next to Islam was another of his misjudgments.[67]

It was also a disadvantage for Meyer that but few American universities, among them Yale and Harvard, had chairs for free and unhindered research into Calvinistic Churches. Perhaps he did not know the English subject-jargon very well either. To be sure, reformed theology as an academic subject was relatively new in

---

[66]Meyer, 199.

[67]Plural marriage practiced by some Mormon leaders, as he alleges, can in no way be compared to keeping a harem of certain Moslems. See 2.5 and 3.5 below.

Germany as well. It had been initiated around 1847 when Salt Lake City was founded. The chair at the University of Erlangen in the Kingdom of Bavaria defended the "right of Jesus Christ in the Church even against prideful defiance of the human establishment of religion and church."[68] The self-contemplation of reformed theology in Germany is exactly as old as the solidification of the central concern of the Church of Jesus Christ of Latter-day Saints.

But even today it can be appreciated that questions and criticism arose concerning the translation of "ancient reformed Egyptian hieroglyphics" which Joseph Smith saw on the plates but which could no longer be examined because the prophet had to return the plates. Who in this border region of magical-supernatural Christianity could solve the puzzle or answer the questions? A theological enemy would conclude that the prophet had a psychopathic disposition[69] while an adherent would praise the prophet's divine prophetic gift and shield him from adversaries.

1.5 The Evaluation of Mormonism and its Esteem in Contemporary Germany

At this point it must be stated that for religious-historical and dogmatic reasons, German theologians reject Mormonism as a heretical, non-Christian new religious organization. The Church of Jesus Christ, on the other hand, considers itself to be uniquely Christian, and for this reason the government's section on Sects of the European Church Authorities fear the Church. In an era that emphasizes Christian social welfare and ecumenical activities,

---

[68]Matthias Freudenberg, "Katholischer König und reformierte Theologie: Vor 150 Jahren Gründung des Lehrstuhls für Reformierte Theologie in Erlangen," *Reformierte KirchenZeitung* [sic], vol. 138, July 15, 1997, 307-309. The *Realencyclopädie für protestantische Theologie und Kirche* is one of the most significant publication in this subject area.

[69]M. H. A. van der Valk, *De profet der Mormonen, Joseph Smith* (Rotterdam, 1921).

authors of reference books brazenly and presumptiously make the following un-Christian recommendation: "Under no circumstances must church-owned facilities be shared with the Mormons."[70] Ironically this attitude can be considered to be a step forward since the beginning of the First World War when any missionary activity of the Church was "always immediately suppressed by the police".[71]

If missionary activities continue long enough, the success of a faith can in part be demonstrated by numbers. In 1860 German and Swiss branches of the Church had about 1000 members. Around 1900 there were about 1200 members in Germany[72], 7000 in 1918 , nearly 10,000 in 1933, and close to 14,000 in 1939. Starting in 1933 while the national socialist ruled Germany, but certainly from 1935 to 1945 the LDS Church activities "were restricted" to put it mildly.[73] As early as spring of 1939 the central administration of the Church in Salt Lake City worried about the safety of the missionaries in Germany and evacuated them to neighboring countries. Despite these adversaties, according to their critic R. Hauth,[74] the Mormons continued to convert approximately one hundred persons per year.

After the Second World War church life of the Latter-day Saints was consolidated to the extent that several chapels could be erected. This development became possible because the Church of Jesus Christ of Latter-day Saints in the 1950s was given full legal status as "Körperschaft des öffentlichen Rechts." In 1985 the [East] German Democratic Republic permitted the Church to build a beautiful

---

[70] *"Mormonen"*, section 3.13, 406, *Handbuch religiöser Gemeinschaften* (Gütersloh, 1993).

[71] K. Heussi, *Kompendium der Kirchengeschichte*, 12th ed. (Tübingen, 1960), 496.

[72] Worldwide the Church had 236 000 members.

[73] *Handbuch religiöser Gemeinschaften*, 393. Helmuth Huebner, a seventeen year old Mormon youth from Hamburg was executed in Berlin for "antifascist agitation".

[74] *Die Mormonen*, 68.

temple in the old Saxon silver mining town of Freiberg. The Chairman of the Council of State, Erich Honecker, personally had granted permission. In 1987 the Frankfurt-Temple in Friedrichsdorf near the Main-River metropolis was dedicated. In 1992 there were about 36,000 members in the reunited Germany, in 1995 about 38,000.[75] After German reunification on October 3, 1990, it was expected that membership of the LDS Church "would have unimpeded possibilities for rapid growth."[76] That is a rather euphemistic statement. If, for example, an American scholar, not a German citizen, would succeed in submitting his inaugural dissertation and if he were then accepted for a teaching position at a German university without revealing that he is an active Mormon or Freemason, his permission to lecture, the famous *venia legendi*, could be revoked.[77]

At the present time two diametrically opposed books are in print that deal with Mormonism as a religious phenomenon in the world and in Germany. One is a sociological account which portrays the development of Mormonism up to our day like a very serious pioneer saga. The author describes this development as the path to enlightenment in the history of Daguerrotypie.[78] The other was written

---

[75]*Handbuch*, 402. These figures are confirmed in the *Fischer Weltalmanach* of 1996. Bruce van Orden's *The Latter-day Saints in Europe* also contains these figures.

[76]*Die Mormonen,* 70.

[77]According to the *Reichs Habilitations Ordnung* which has not been revoked. Consult Franz Senger, ed. *Reichs Habilitations Ordnung* (Berlin 1939), 29 and 43. Also W. Sellert, "Zur Problematik der Habilitation ...", *Zeitschrift für Rechtspolitik*, Vol. 5, 1972, 68-72. W. Kremer, T. Kelm, "Mitgliedschaft in neuen Religions- und Weltanschauungsgemeinschaften", *Neue Juristische Wochenschrift*, 1997, Heft 13, 832-837. Consult also the Basic Recommendations [Grundsatzempfehlungen] of the "Enquete-Kommission" in "Sogenannte Sekten und Psychogruppen" of the German Parliament, June 1998. *Drucksachen.* 13/10950. I am indebted to my colleague Thomas G. Alexander of BYU for this latter information.

[78]Douglas Tobler and Nelson Wadsworth, *Der Weg zum Licht. Die Geschichte der Mormonen in Bildern und Texten* (Kehl am Rhein, 1987).

by the pastor and "commissioner for sects" [Sektenbeauftragter] Dr. Hauth as a guide and "book of advice" to "unmask" Mormonism as a dangerous sect which is based on a "product of imagination", the Book of Mormon.

At this point I will pause and state a decisive difference in the perception of this religious community that depends on revelation. The Church of Jesus Christ of Latter-day Saints is completely integrated in U.S. American life because it has consistently endeavored not to lose its profile and originality, and because it did not have to abandon its specific deviations from the non-Catholic church norm. Thus it has developed in Utah, and in other parts of the world, into a church with a unique spectrum. Inside the Church one can observe a struggle for direction from a golden middle, an avant-garde and a rearguard[79] as in every other Christian church as well. In German theological literature there exists nothing — unless it has been previously conceived by an American or Frenchman — that is comparable in formal elegance to the non-Mormon Massimo Introvigne, in seriousness to Tobler and in genuine imagery to Wadsworth. The heritage transmitted by these writers is simply ignored by German critics as if it were not part of the LDS pioneer accomplishment. Despite the two temples and a considerable number of meritorious members in Germany, the Mormon Church has remained a foreign body in public and judicial fields and is regarded with distrust and rejection. Why? Because it is still suspected to be a sect. The general public, and more specifically German theological circles, do not permit the LDS Church to take its deserved place in the family of Christian churches. Yet it is a legal public corporation (Körperschaft des öffentlichen Rechts), and it serves people in a way that is certainly considered to be Christian in nature.

---

[79]Carefully observed by M. Introvigne, *Les Mormons*, note 27, 147ff.

2. The Quest for the New Jerusalem in America

Originally "the finger of the Lord"[1] had "appointed the temple lot" and suggested the rectangular[2] form of the ground plan "portrayed upon" the shape of a tile. But now, because of the **new** gathering of the "saints", a New Jerusalem had to be found. Where was this Zion to be located?

An in-depth basic understanding of Mormonism is not exactly made easy, since geographic misunderstandings still exist today. For example, the editors of the most recent *Länderbericht USA*[3] of the German Federal Printing Office assert that the Mormons, who in 1838 were driven out of Missouri, were persecuted in the "East" of the country. Actually, however, at that time Missouri was located in the West of the country. The Western frontier began in Missouri along the Mississippi River. West of the river, Indian country began, and areas even further to the West were Mexican Territory. The publishers of modern German travel literature commit another error even though they attempt to rectify the former. They situate Utah in the Southwest of the United States.[4] In the 1840s of the 19th century, Missouri was located on the Western frontier of the United States and the Utah Basin along the Great Salt Lake in Mexico, i.e. in a foreign country. Today residents of Utah consider themselves Westerners.

---

[1]Doctrine and Covenants 84:3-4.

[2]Eziekel 4:1.

[3]Willi Paul Adams, ed., et alii, *Amerika*, vol. 1, updated ed. Bundeszentrale für politische Bildung, Schriftenreihe, vol. 293/I (Bonn, 1993), 28.

[4]Volker Mehnert, *Südwesten: Utah, New Mexico, Arizona, Süd-Colorado/US* (München, 1995). Manfred Braunger, *USA-Südwest. Richtig Reisen* (Köln, 1996).

To escape from total annihilation,[5] about 7500 believers left the Western frontier of the United States in 1848 and settled temporarily in contested Indian Territory. They sought final refuge in the desert at the foot of the Rocky Mountains. 1650 people reached that destination seventeen months later, including the time it took to travel to "Winter Quarters". I will give a more detailed account of the reasons for the expulsion in 2.2 below.

At any rate, the Exodus-Mormons had succeeded to begin their trek before the outbreak of the Mexican War in May 1846 and to end it two months before the American conquest of Mexico City.[6] Catching sight of the vast expanse of the Great Salt Lake Valley on July 24, 1847, the pioneer leader and Apostle of the Mormon Church, Brigham Young (1801-1877), uttered the now famous words: "This is the right place."[7] This utterance is of particular religious significance since it represents a fulfillment of the Prophet Joseph Smith's revelation.[8] A city previously spiritually conceived, was at this moment in time actually founded. Today the metropolitan area of Salt Lake City[9] is the largest area of concentration between Alberta,

---

[5]In 1838 Lilburg Boggs, the Governor of Missouri, had issued his infamous expulsion and annihilation order which was widely publicized.

[6]The Mormon Battalion distinguished itself with exemplary bravery by completing the longest infantry march in U.S. military history (1800 kilometers) from Fort Leavenworth, via Santa Fé, to San Diego, Mexico. Tobler-Wadsworth, *Der Weg zum Licht,* 131.

[7]The huge area which later was called "Deseret", encompassing the modern states of Utah, Nevada, Southeastern California, Arizona, and parts of Oregon and Colorado, was officially ceded by Mexico to the United States on February 2, 1848 in the Treaty of Guadelupe Hidalgo. These events are often confused by German writers. The exodus from Winter Quarters to the Salt Lake Valley did not take place in 1846 as G. Moltmann and W. Lindig contend in *USA-Ploetz,* (82) but in 1847, and a federal state called Utah (87) did not yet exist in 1850.

[8]A Widtsoe, *Joseph Smith: Seeker after Truth* (1996), Chapter 51.

[9]Today, the city proper of Salt Lake City is located along the shores of the Great Salt Lake and has 171,000 inhabitants (more than 50% Mormon), while more than a million people live in the greater metropolitan area. In the year 2002

Canada and Arizona, and between San Francisco, California and Denver, Colorado.

The advance guard, led by Orson Pratt, which had been sent ahead to find this "sacred place", discovered in the valley "rich, black, slightly sandy soil". Immediately after their arrival they dedicated the land between the Wasatch Mountain Range and the Jordan River[10] to the Lord, staked out vegetable beds and fields and planted potatoes, beans, corn and buckwheat. On the first weekend, after Brigham Young had arrived, they dug irrigation ditches.

The first Sunday, July 25, was a day of rest. The next day woodcutters were dispatched into the surrounding mountains to look for trees suitable for building material. On Tuesday a provisional smithy was fired up with charcoal, and the first horseshoes were made. Within a week eight acres had been planted and an additional five plowed by thirteen plows and harrowed by three harrows, pulled by proven oxen, steered by competent pioneer fists, guided by a natural and hardened self-discipline, and protected by a strong faith.

The first centrally located main building was a provisional bower. Already on August 10, Orson Pratt laid out the temple square which was limited to two and a half acres. A fort was quickly erected and "houses" were built in the Spanish adobe style: wet clay was mixed with fiber material, pressed in a brick mold and dried in the sun. This manner of construction is different from the earlier "triangular" style of Fort St. James in Virginia (1607) or the Arx Carolina in Florida (1671). It follows rather the "four cornered" style of the Old Testament with log huts[11] on the inside of the settlement. These huts

---

the Olympic Winter Games will be held in this area, an event which will accord this beautiful, well planned city international fame which it so richly deserves.

[10]The pioneers named the river after the biblical River Jordan in Palestine.

[11]It must be remembered that the pioneers did not have any kind of modern construction machinery.

were not attached to the outside walls.[12] The log cabins were built for survival in the winter which fortunately was surprisingly mild in 1847-48.

More and more Mormons[13] followed the first main group so that food quickly became scarce. From the Ute Indians the settlers learned to dig up and prepare sego roots. Brigham Young believed that it was "less expensive to trade with the Indians than to fight with them". Only three years had passed when Chief Walkara was baptized a member of the Church in 1850. Half of his tribe, about 250 men and women, followed his example. In the fall of 1847, Parley Pratt had already encountered the Indians as predominantly honest horse traders. He reports that the Ute Indians "were good-looking, brave and very intelligent". They wanted to learn as much as possible from the Mormons, and "they even wanted to be united as one people with us and cultivate the earth as we had shown them". This pacification policy was undoubtedly motivated by a religious conviction, for the Mormons intended to put into praxis their missionary zeal, or stated differently: the Indian Mission was an essential part of the Mormons' Christianity. Thus during the first years, peace was established between the settlers and the main Ute tribe and was maintained for a while.

It already becomes obvious from these introductory remarks that the early Mormon settlement idea was characterized by special considerations: the available forces were bundled, given a religious foundation and employed cooperatively. While many other American one-purpose settlements, overnight villages (for example in Oklahoma), and collections of huts built by speculators lacked any

---

[12]The wooden palisade of Fort Salt Lake was 26 inches wide and 8 feet high. With the exception of two vertical gates the palisade surrounded the entire inner area. S. George Ellsworth, *Utah Heritage* (1977), 150-165, 154 and 163.

[13]In the second winter of 1848-49 already more than 4500 settlers had arrived in the valley.

kind of planning, Salt Lake "City" was carefully planned out from the beginning.

2.1 Mormon Settlements According to the Plan of Zion

Urgency was of the essence. If the long arm of the United States Congress was not soon to be felt in this new settlement, positive facts had to be established. A long history of planning had preceded the actual building of Salt Lake City. Streets and houses had to be built on a grid pattern, and the entire city layout had to be surveyed in rectangular form. In the planning of every city founded by Mormons, two inspired ideas played an important role: first, planning beforehand the restoration of a divinely inspired New Jerusalem,[14] or the City of Zion, and second the actual realization of the plans for a new city populated by faithful believers.

Before the great forerunner of the Mormon "Kingdom" on earth in Missouri could be established, the Prophet Joseph Smith had sent the model plan of a prototype "City of Zion" (the New Jerusalem) to Jackson County, Missouri. He had selected a city with the name of Independence which today is an Eastern suburb of Kansas City. The plans called "plat" are preserved and extensively explained in two volumes[15] by Professor John W. Reps, the Princeton expert of US architectural history.

The basis for the founding of cities in Smith's concept is neither the exploitation of natural resources nor the profit motive but rather the

---

[14]"The Civitas Dei which St. Augustine contrasts with the civitas populi comes to mind. *The City of God* (New York, 1958), introduction by Etienne Gilson. Also Doctrine and Covenants 42 and 62 (1831).

[15]*Cities of the American West* (Princeton, 1979), 288ff. and *The Making of Urban America: A History of City Planning in the United States* (1992), 466ff. For the symbolism consult Steven L. Olson, "Joseph Smith's Concept of the City of Zion", ed. S. E. Black and Charles D. Tate, *Joseph Smith, the Prophet the Man* (1993), 203-211.

fulfillment of a spiritual commission. The locality was determined by prophetic insight. The impetus for the plan was provided by Leviticus 35:4-5 in the Old Testament, and this prophecy had been taken up anew in 3 Nephi 22.[16] On the other hand, the prophet had visited New York City in 1832 and admired how the streets and houses were ordered by a grid concept which pleased "the language of his heart". He had received a similar impression when he studied the ground plan of the City of Philadelphia with its quadrants of High Street (South-North) and Broad Street (East-West). A city plan, as for example for New Harmony in Indiana, was the basis for "Father" George Rapps's (1757-1847) spiritual-utopian, geometric planning energy. Since the young prophet was acquainted with the plan of Harmony, Pennsylvania he was able to consider the problems of city planning seriously.

An 1833 plat with handwritten instructions dictated by Joseph Smith to his scribe has been preserved.[17] In these instructions he notes that the prototype of the new Zion was to have 15,000 to 20,000 inhabitants or "souls", as they were commonly referred to at that time. Initially "Zion" was to consist of 1000 lots, large enough for a family of 15 to 20 persons. Such a high number of persons surpasses the usual concept even for families of lower class German immigrants in the 18th century. They consisted ordinarily of no more than 7-12 persons.[18] J. W. Reps asks himself why Joseph Smith in 1833 believed that families would be so large, but he does not have a definitive answer.[19] In my estimation, Reps asks the right question. Is it because of planned or envisioned plural marriage? The central block of the

---

[16]See Parley P. Pratt, *A Voice of Warning* for the description of biblical cities and *The Essential Parley P. Pratt,* Classics in Mormon Thought Series, No. 1, 1990, intro. by Peter L. Crawley.

[17]John W. Reps, *The Making of Urban America*, figure 278, 470.

[18]Christian Gellinek, *Northwest Germany in Northeast America* (Münster, 1997), 9. In the 17th century families on average had up to 14 persons.

[19]*The Making of Urban America,* 467. R. L. Bushman, *Making Space for the Mormons*, 4-16.

city and the three inner blocks reserved for religious buildings were to comprise 49 quadrants, one square mile in total area. Unusually wide streets were planned, the main streets to be 40 meters wide, the side streets 25. Houses were set to be seven meters back from the street. The building material was to be stone and brick. Copies of this prototype city were to be constructed according to this spacious model. "For this is the City of Zion", can be read in the handwritten postscript added in the margins of the plan for Zion, dictated by Joseph Smith to his scribe.[20]

This plan was not yet put into practice in the city of Independence, Missouri in 1830/31, but with a few adjustments when the city of Nauvoo, Illinois was built 1839-1844.[21] Until 1877, Brigham Young, following the slightly modified (and adjusted to local conditions) "Plan of Zion", founded Salt Lake City (1847ff.), Bountiful (1848ff.), and Provo (1849ff.) in Utah as well as twenty additional settlements in the huge area which was to be the State of Deseret.[22]

Behind these impressive numbers, one recognizes the spiritually driven intention of the prophet to plan for secular housing which Brigham Young, who succeeded him as prophet and leader of the Church, brought to fruition. It also becomes obvious from these considerations that only the location of the planned city was to be revealed but not the actual execution of the city plan. The most important point of the city planning prophet was that a single house was to be erected on a lot with a lawn in front and a vegetable garden in back. It was anticipated that vegetables thus harvested were

---

[20]Reps, look underneath the directional entry "West", figure 9.1, "Plan of the City of Zion".

[21]For initial problems in building the city, consult *Cities of the American West*, 289. In 1842, when Joseph Smith was still alive, Nauvoo is reported to have had 7000 inhabitants, 297-298 and illustration 9.5.

[22]He also caused at least eighty small cities to be founded in the Utah Basin. See *Cities of the American West*, 313; G. Lowry Nelson Jr., *The Mormon Village (*Salt Lake City, 1952).

perhaps not sufficient for the family and therefore additional food was to be grown by common labor on farms outside of town. Farmers, just like artisans, should rest and sleep in town, not outside, separated from Zion.

Let us now investigate which elements of this city planning were typically American and which characteristically Mormon. The grid concept and separate houses for each family is standard. The idea of a front garden, according to Reps,[23] was not totally unknown, but neither were front gardens widespread. Situating the main church building in the center of town was practiced in New England, for example in New Haven, Connecticut. Uniquely Mormon is the turning of all directional axes of the house in every block and the turning of every block itself by 90 degrees.. This is obvious from the plan and from the actual construction of such a city. Perhaps this may be explained by the unusually high number of individuals (15-20) anticipated for each family. Somehow the prophet must have thought already in 1833, ten years before its actual proclamation, of the fruits of plural marriage. By turning each planned house on its axis by 90 degrees, one could not look directly into the windows of the facing house. Thus privacy for the family was assured at least to some extent. It seems that because of the high number of persons per family and the turning of houses, two to three wives were anticipated per household by the planning spirit Joseph Smith. Preplanning might even have prepared the way for a future revelation.

Thus, on account of the prototypical City of New Jerusalem or Zion, we note architecturally anticipated population planning. Because of the immediacy of the plans and their explanation by the prophet, it appears that such city planning, occurring before the revelation of July 12, 1843,[24] was not regarded to be anachronistic but rather as

---

[23]*Cities*, 290.

[24]According to Doctrine and Covenants 132:61-62, "a plurality of wives" is only acceptable "if the Lord commands it", the latter as noted in the introduction to the section of the German edition, 236/237.

not attend church regularly.[7] It seems that Lucy Mack had not been baptized as a child because for a while her parents were indentured servants. During his life, Lucy's father had several "inspired visionary dreams" which were probably an expression of his dissatisfaction with local Protestant denominations. The parents of the prophet seem to have been convinced that their efforts to live as obedient Christians deserved to be rewarded. This attitude can be interpreted as "moderately Calvinistic" or "Arminian".[8] Joseph's father was a Methodist in name only, his wife was a non-conformist.

In the summer, Joseph Smith, Sr., worked on the farm, in the winter as cooper and part-time teacher. Young Joseph had not yet attended school in 1812[9] when a typhoid epidemic broke out in the area and affected the family. Joseph became quite ill, and eventually the illness settled in the bone of his left leg. As a consequence of a festering infection and several incisions, the boy suffered excruciating pain. The doctors advised that the leg should be amputated, but Joseph and his family refused. Finally a competent surgeon who had been trained at Dartmouth College, in a daring operation removed part of the bone without giving the boy any anesthetic. The seven year old Joseph bravely endured the brutal procedure. His father held him in his arms and tried to comfort his little son as best he could. Joseph's mother was not able to watch the operation, but fled outside and prayed for her child. After three years, the leg finally healed. Until the end of his life Joseph was left with a slight limp.[10]

Joseph Smith, Jr., undoubtedly learned a basic knowledge of English and religion from his parents and from his older brothers and sister. During his three year period of convalescence he had ample time to study the King-James-Bible which did not include the apocrypha. He

---

[7] Bushman, *The Beginning*, 5.

[8] Bushman, 27. It can also be called Universalistic or "Grotian".

[9] Later in his youth he attended school irregularly in Chenango, Broome County. Bushman, 215 endnote 107.

[10] Bushman, 33-35.

is said to have favored the Epistle of James which Protestants considered to be unorthodox and poetic. Pro-Arminians, however, regarded it as fairly orthodox. Joseph also read books written for boys by Stephen Borroughs and stories about Captain Robert Kidd.[11] His mother, his uncle Jason, and his aunt Lovis Mack were creative people, and thus we may assume that the active and vivacious family followed extraordinary religious events with great interest.

We know that the young man earned his keep with hard farm labor and other occasional work, and that he was quite capable and adroit.[12] When he was twenty-one years old he was over six feet tall, had long legs, a muscular body, broad shoulders, an oval head, hazel eyes, light brown hair, and bushy eyebrows.[13] He fell in love with an attractive and intelligent young school teacher by the name of Emma Hale, the daughter of the property owner Isaac Hale and his wife Elizabeth. Emma also was tall, had even features and beautiful black hair. Joseph and his father had accepted work in a silver mine near Harmony, Pennsylvania, and there Joseph met Emma. Since Joseph was not one of the local boys but a stranger in the area, Isaac Hale did not want his daughter to marry Joseph, so Joseph borrowed a black suit and a horse and buggy and eloped with Emma to get married in Manchester in January 1827. Later Joseph was reconciled with his in-laws. By the way, Emma was also a Mayflower descendant via her mother whose maiden name was Lewis.

It is of interest to note that young Smith was a married man when he was permitted to lift the golden plates from the Hill Cumorah. His young wife was his confidante and the first person, outside of his immediate family, to believe in him. From the end of 1827 until the beginning of 1828 Joseph, who considered himself a poor stylist, dictated part of the text of the Book of Mormon to his pregnant wife.

---

[11] M. R. Werner, *Brigham Young* (New York, 1925), 20-21.

[12] Bushman, 69.

[13] Bushman, 77. Backman, 149.

She gave birth to a child on June 15, 1828, but to their great sorrow the child died on the same day.[14]

In the meantime Joseph had become acquainted with Martin Harris, a well-to-do neighboring farmer who became interested in Joseph's religious convictions. They discussed the publication of a "golden bible", as the text was called by neighbors, and the possible resulting financial loss. Harris agreed to be the second scribe. When the manuscript was partially completed, Joseph refused permission to have people inspect the plates. He felt that it was too early to show them. He did allow Harris, however, to take some of the hieroglyphics which he and Emma had copied, for inspection to New York City. Harris showed the "caractors" and their translation to Dr. Charles Anthon (1797-1867), a professor of classical philology at Columbia College.[15] Harris reported to the prophet that Anthon had considered the characters to be authentic and their translation correct. This report satisfied Smith and Harris, but not Mrs. Harris who insisted on seeing the 116 original pages of translation which her husband had carefully written down. Joseph Smith never saw those pages again. It is generally assumed that Mrs. Harris burned the manuscript in her fireplace.[16] Because of this incident the translation was temporarily halted.

In the spring of 1829 Smith made the acquaintance of Oliver Cowdery (1806-1850) a compatriot from Vermont who had some training in legal matters, experience in newspaper writing and a fine writing style. He became excited about Smith's activities and wanted to be part of the work that seemed to him to be pleasing in the sight of the Lord. Emma and her brother continued to help occasionally with the translation, but beginning in the spring of 1829 Cowdery was the

---

[14]According to Hill the child was named Alva, 74-75. Bushman states it was Alvin, 91.

[15]Joseph Smith, ed. *The Times and Seasons*, III, 13 (Nauvoo 1842). Bushman, 87 ff. Hill, 75 ff.

[16]Bushman, 92 endnote 41.

primary scribe. When Joseph had completed most of the translation work in May 1829 he realized that he did not have divine authority to act in the name of God and administer the ordinances of the gospel. In answer to fervent prayer, the resurrected John the Baptist appeared to both Joseph and Oliver and ordained them to the priesthood.[17] Following his instructions the two men baptized each other in the Susquehanna river. Later both men received the Melchizedek Priesthood, and Joseph was called the first elder of the church, Oliver the second.[18]

The next important convert was John Whitmer (1802-1878)[19] a farmer and cattleman who also acted as scribe for the prophet. In the spring of 1830 the manuscript was ready for printing. Joseph, only twenty-four years old, had completed a book manuscript which eventually was to be distributed worldwide. He had been assisted by his wife, his family, relatives, friends, a neighbor, and two converts, some of whom had acted as scribes. The Book of Mormon was dictated by a lay theologian to several believers whose faith in divine guidance remained unshaken during their participation as writers.

On account of continuous work on the revealed record, a "truth seeker" who had to keep the plates hidden from curious and designing persons, had actually found the truth. With the help of the Book of Mormon, Joseph Smith gathered around him a group of believers who had overcome their initial doubts. His neighbor, Martin Harris, helped pay for the printing with a considerable amount of money.[20] Joseph Smith inspired others with his enthusiasm and

---

[17]Doctrine and Covenants 13. Joseph Smith – History 68-73.

[18]Doctrine and Covenants 20:2-3. Joseph Smith – History 72. In 1841 Hyrum Smith replaced Oliver Cowdery. Philipp R. Legg, *Oliver Cowdery*.

[19]Son of the Pennsylvanian Peter Whitmer (1773-1854) and his wife Mary Musselmann, who was of German descent. Five of their eight children were witnesses to the truthfulness of the Book of Mormon, see 3.1 above.

[20]Doctrine and Covenants 19:26. By revelation Martin was commanded to "impart freely to the printing of the Book of Mormon".

succeeded in conceiving a religious denomination and step by step in founding and perfecting a new church.

To further clarify the events leading up to the founding of the Church it seems to me essential to refer in some detail to the prophet's own account of his life's history.[21] In this account the last verses of the fourth chapter of Malachi are paraphrased and "strengthened". With these scriptures the prophet points out the large lacuna apparent in the King-James-Bible because of the Calvinistic deletion of the apocryphal books. The last verse of the Old Testament states that the earth will be smitten "with a curse" at Christ's last coming, unless the prophet Elijah will "turn the hearts of the fathers to the children, and the heart of the children to their fathers".[22]

At this point the coauthor-translator would like to add a paragraph with his interpretation of the Malachi text. The angel Moroni appeared to Joseph Smith and in addition to various instructions quoted from the last chapter of Malachi[23] "with a little variation from the way it reads in our Bibles". He states that before the Second Coming, i.e. "the great and dreadful day of the Lord", the priesthood will be restored which will have the authority to officiate in the sacred ordinances of the temple. He continues that the prophet Elijah, who held the keys of sealing work in ancient times, will return these keys so that "the heart of the children [shall be turned] to their fathers".[24] Today, indeed, the hearts of the Latter-day Saints are turned to their forefathers, and they are diligently gathering information about them from old church records and other documents. With this information they are able to go to the temple and have themselves sealed to their

---

[21]Joseph Smith – History 36-39 in the Pearl of Great Price.

[22]Malachi 4:6.

[23]Joseph Smith – History 36-39.

[24]Elijah did return on April 3, 1836. He appeared to Joseph Smith and Oliver Cowdery in the Kirtland Temple and committed the keys of temple work into their hands. "... by this ye may know that the great and dreadful day of the Lord is near." D&C 110:13-16.

ancestors so that they will be united as families in the resurrection. The information gathered is deposited in the largest family history library (in Salt Lake City) in the world, and is available to anyone free of charge, now even on the internet.

On April 6, 1830, eleven days after the publication of the Book of Mormon, Joseph Smith assembled friends in Peter Whitmer's log cabin in Fayette, Seneca County, New York. After prayer, confirmings, blessings and the Lord's Supper, Joseph Smith legally[25] founded the Church of Christ, as it was initially called. During this first meeting, Joseph, his older brother Hyrum, Peter Whitmer,[26] David Whitmer,[27] and Oliver Cowdery were ordained and confirmed elders. Joseph Knight, Sr., (1772-1847), an early disciple and generous friend of the prophet, reports that Joseph Smith was overjoyed when his father and Martin Harris were baptized in a nearby stream that evening.[28]

A few days before this carefully planned meeting, Joseph Smith had laid, so to speak, the cornerstone with the revelation recorded in section 20 of the Doctrine and Covenants. This revelation confirms the prophet as an ordained apostle and first elder of the new church and outlines its organization and the duties of apostles, elders, priests, teachers, and deacons.[29] Beginning with the founding date of the Church, Joseph Smith and his assistants began to establish a theocratically oriented church hierarchy on three levels:

---

[25]"...the Church of Christ ...being regularly organized and established agreeable to the laws of the country ..." Doctrine and Covenants 20:1.

[26]A tailor by profession, he was one of the eight witnesses of the Book of Mormon. See 3.1 above.

[27]He was converted in 1829 and together with Martin Harris and Oliver Cowdery was one of the three witnesses of the Book of Mormon. Compare D&C 14. He was excommunicated in 1838.

[28]Hill, 107.

[29]D&C 20.

As we have already seen, on one level we are dealing with the establishment of LDS communities. On account of constant persecutions new towns and areas were founded and dedicated: Ohio as the Land of Zion (1831); Jackson County, Missouri (1839) from which the Saints were expelled because of Governor Boggs's infamous extermination order; Nauvoo in Illinois (1839); and finally the Salt Lake Valley and communities in the West.

Missionary work is launched on a large scale, at first in England (1837), after that also in Sweden, Germany, Switzerland and other European countries.

Doctrine is firmly established in the new church. The main part of today's Doctrine and Covenants with its collection of revelations and instructions was ready to be printed in November 1831 as the *Book of Commandments*. Its publication was, however, delayed when the printing press was destroyed by enemies of the Church. The book was enlarged by necessary additions, and a new, revised version was accepted and published in 1835.[30] Three especially noteworthy doctrines contained in the book are:

A. baptism by proxy for deceased ancestors, announced on August 15, 1840,
B. the thirteen Articles of Faith, published on March 1, 1842,
C. polygyny, announced on July 12, 1843.

Except for polygyny, Joseph Smith first proclaimed these doctrines orally – according to witnesses – in a mature, clear voice. He had mastered a speaking style which allowed him to announce a new revelation without any hesitation and without reviewing, making changes or corrections. The written texts were, however, carefully

---

[30] The twelve apostles of the Church added their testimony "to the truth of the Book of Doctrine and Covenants".

reviewed and revised before their publication.[31] Since I already discussed the Articles of Faith and polygyny in 3.2 above, I will now briefly comment on baptism by proxy for the dead. A revelation received by Joseph Smith on January 21, 1836[32] in the Kirtland Ohio Temple states that "all who have died without a knowledge of this gospel, who would have received it if they had been permitted to tarry, shall be heirs of the celestial kingdom of God". Beginning in 1841 such baptisms were performed in rivers, for example in the Mississippi, and later in the Nauvoo Temple. This ordinance developed from a "service of love" into a "saving ordinance".[33] Three Bible scriptures are the foundation for baptism for the dead. Some are more convincing than others. The first is found in Malachi 4:5-6, the second in 1 Corinthians 15:29[34], and the third in 1 Peter 3:18, written by Paul.[35] To me the verses in Malachi do not appear directly to refer to baptism for the dead. The scripture in Corinthians, however, undoubtedly indicates that the early Christians at the time of Paul, and most likely later also,[36] performed proxy baptisms for their dead. Paul neither condones nor rejects this ordinance. The scripture in 1 Peter could be indirectly interpreted to mean that the dead who are "quickened by the Spirit" are made alive in the realm of the dead. In other words the crucified Christ descends as a living spirit from the sphere of mortality into the realm of the dead where disobedient angels wait. If forgotten angels or spirits should be among them including some that had never been baptized, it would be a loving idea to think that baptism for these dead could replace baptism among the living. The possibility that in this manner a beloved

---

[31]Hill, 141.

[32]D&C 137:7-10.

[33]Even the antagonist Hauth admits as much on page 139 in *Die Mormonen.*

[34]"Else what shall they do which are baptized for the dead, if the dead rise not at all? Why are they then baptized for the dead?"

[35]Compare also D&C 128:15-18.

[36]Ernst Dinkler, *Religion in Geschichte und Gegenwart*, vol. VI (Tübingen, 1962), 958, states that gnostic Christians still performed baptisms for the dead in the 6th century. Officially the practice had been forbidden since 397.

ancestor or a child that died without having been baptized could be saved is indeed a most comforting thought.[37] He who does not forget the dead, reduces their suffering. The prophet asks if we "can be made perfect" without our dead?[38] To him baptism for the living and for the dead is a simile for the resurrection.[39] Is it merely a gnostic veil hiding the resurrection or perhaps rather a simile of universal neighborly love?

Again, the original author permits the coauthor-translator to comment in the following paragraph. In the Epistle of Peter referred to above, the writer comments that during the three days before his resurrection, Jesus Christ "being put to death in the flesh but quickened by the Spirit" went into the realm of the dead and "preached unto the spirits in prison". A living person has a physical body and an immortal spirit. At death the body is buried – in Christ's case for only three days – and the spirit proceeds to the spirit world, waiting there for the resurrection when it will be reunited with a perfect and glorified resurrected body, as Christ was after his return from the spirit world.[40] A modern revelation, received by the prophet Joseph F. Smith on October 3, 1918 and recorded in D&C 138, clarifies the events referred to by Peter. Christ not only preached personally "to them that are dead, that they might be judged according to men in the flesh, but live according to God in the spirit"[41] but organized a missionary program so that the gospel can be taught most effectively in that world also by ordained priesthood members.[42] The good news of the restored gospel of Jesus Christ is for all men, but since most never had the opportunity to hear of it and were never baptized, a vital ordinance without which no person

---

[37]D&C 129 distinguishes between various kinds of angels. I consulted also *The Expositor's Bible Commentary*, vol. 12 (Grand Rapids, 1981), 241-243.

[38]D&C 128:15, 18.

[39]D&C 128:12.

[40]Read the events in the Gospel of St. John 20.

[41]1 Peter 4:6.

[42]D&C 138.

can enter the kingdom of heaven,[43] it would be unfair and unkind for those poor unfortunate souls to be consigned to eternal damnation, as some churches teach.[44] How bright is the light that the restored gospel sheds on this matter, how much hope it provides, and how merciful a gracious God really is. Since in the spirit world the gospel can be preached, but a convert can not be baptized, this ordinance must be performed for him by proxy by a loving relative in the House of the Lord. In this way the relative becomes a kind of "savior" figure as alluded to above.

In 1835 Joseph Smith solidified his authority by organizing the Council of Twelve Apostles. One week later he also instituted the Council of Seventy. These councils confirmed his scriptural canon and sustained the First Elder of the Church as President of the Church, a position which President Smith held uncontested until his martyrdom in 1844.

At the end of 1840 the Governor of Illinois granted Nauvoo, located on the Mississippi river, a city charter. In a few years Nauvoo had as many inhabitants as Chicago. It is no wonder that neighbors became jealous of the Mormons and posed an ever growing danger for them. In 1841 Brigham Young, Orson Pratt, John Taylor, Wilford Woodruff and others returned after a very successful mission in England. By 1842 more than 2,749 new converts joined the citizens of Nauvoo.[45]

During this phase, the powerful, influential President of the Church engaged in several business ventures. He became mayor of the city,

---

[43]John 3:5 "Except a man be born of water and of the Spirit [baptized and confirmed] he can not enter into the kingdom of God."

[44]Martin Luther in his treatise *The Bondage of the Will* chapter VII actually is saddened by the fact that "even the most excellent men" and "the noblest among the Greeks" have no chance ever of salvation.

[45]Hill, 289.

lieutenant general of the Nauvoo Legion,[46] participated as judge in court proceedings, and together with Sidney Rigdon chartered the Bank of Nauvoo. Previously the Bank of Kirtland had failed.[47] Smith also speculated in real estate and purchased a river boat, thus becoming a ship owner like his grandfather Solomon Mack before him. Unfortunately he overextended himself and consequently had to declare personal bankruptcy.

We have noted that Joseph Smith belongs to the guild of persons who limped. Sometimes such men are especially fertile.[48] He and his wife Emma had eight children of their own and adopted two more. Their fourth son, Joseph III, eventually became president of the Reorganized Church of Jesus Christ of Latter-day Saints and died when he was 82 years old. Their eighth son was born five months after the prophet's death and reached the age of 60. The Prophet entered several plural marriages, at first possibly in secret, but he must have been convinced that as prophet he had the natural right to do so.[49] According to Donna Hill's research[50] his wife Emma found it extremely difficult to reconcile herself to polygyny. Such a new arrangement was against her wishes and difficult to abide. Joseph consulted her, however, and eventually she consented.[51] May it suffice at this point to review the material on the subject which Donna Hill presents in her book. Joseph insisted on the privilege to approve plural marriages of chosen apostles and members of the council, and Emma had the right to approve his plural wives. Exceptions to this arrangement are unknown. Donna Hill and I are both astounded that

---

[46]Paintings show him dressed in a fanciful military uniform. The Legion was organized to protect the Saints and their property.

[47]US President Jackson had vetoed the extension of federal guarantees which contributed to the bank failure.

[48]Peter L. Hays, *The Limping Hero*, New York University Press, 1971.

[49]Please refer to 2.5 above.

[50]Hill, 346-361. See also L. J. Arrington, *Brigham Young*, Appendix. C. M. Werner, *Brigham, Young*, 142. *Historical Record*, Salt Lake City, May 1887.

[51]In D&C 132:51-56 Emma is requested to support her husband. It seems apparent that she had given her consent previously.

no descendants of the prophet's plural marriages are known. There is no way of knowing why not [except that he probably did not consummate some of them!]. The names of the following fifteen women who have been "officially recognized" as plural wives of the prophet are known:

1. {Name not authenticated, possibly} Fanny Alger[s], in Kirtland 1835/37.
2. Louisa Be[a]man, on April 5, 1841. She was later married to Brigham Young and had five children with him.
3. Zina D. Huntington, on October 27, 1841. She later became Brigham Young's wife.
4. Prescindia L. Huntington, Zina's sister, on December 11, 1841. She had visited Joseph in Liberty Jail in February 1839. Later she became the wife of Heber C. Kimball.
5. Olive Grey Frost. Later became Brigham Young's wife. She died 1845.
6. Mary E. Rollins, in 1842.
7. Eliza Roxey Snow,[52] educator, poetess, on June 29, 1842. She later was married to Brigham Young.
8. Sarah Ann Whitney, on July 27, 1842.
9. Emily D. Partridge, on March 4, 1843. She later became the wife of Brigham Young and bore him seven children.
10. Eliza M. Partridge, in March 1843.
11. Sarah Lawrence, an orphan from Canada, in 1843.
12. Maria Lawrence, Sarah's twin sister. She later married Brigham Young. She died 1847.
13. Lucy Walker, in May 1843. She later married Heber Kimball. They had 9 children.
14. Elmera Johnson, on April 5, 1843.
15. Helen Mar Kimball, daughter of Heber Kimball, in May 1843.[53]

---

[52]The sister of Lorenzo Snow, the fifth president of the Church from 1898-1901.

When this new doctrine was introduced to the High Council of the Church on August 12, 1843, a storm of indignation broke lose among the non-Mormon neighbors, especially in Illinois. On account of the constant deprecations and persecutions of the prophet as well as the lack of finances, Joseph Smith must have felt harassed and trapped in a hopeless situation. The traumatic effect which the plural marriage issue must have had on the psyche of the prophet, on the innermost core of his "persona", is difficult to assess.

During the last three years of his life, Joseph Smith must have carefully balanced his calling as church official and spiritual leader. Keeping these two constantly in proper balance must have been extremely strenuous. Besides all his ceremonial duties he probably had little time for his private life. Referring to sections 127 to 133 in the Doctrine and Covenants it becomes quite apparent that he concentrated his main thoughts and efforts on the themes of death and resurrection and on the relationship between the living and the dead. In 5.3 below I will return to the religious philosophy which was revealed to the prophet towards the end of his life.

Like the beleaguered Roman general Caesar, Joseph Smith who was encircled on all sides, decided that his best defense was a good offence. Consequently in the spring of 1844, after he had moved into his beautiful "Mansion House", he declared his candidacy for the highest political office of the nation: the presidency of the United States of America. As his vice presidential candidate he chose Sidney Rigdon, and both plunged into the battle for votes. I will not venture into the details of the campaign: the support of Brigham Young and other Church leaders, mistakes that might have been made, and

---

[53]M. Werner names an additional 13 women who supposedly were sealed to Joseph Smith between 1841 and 1844. Fawn F. Brodie, *No Man Knows my History: The Life of Joseph Smith*, 2nd ed., 1986, Appendix C, counts 48 plural wives. Todd Compton, *In Sacred Loneliness: The Plural Wives of Joseph Smith* (Salt Lake City, 1997), does not include Elmera Johnson but adds 20 additional names.

whether the prophet's candidacy was pure political calculation. All this has been amply discussed by competent scholars. Of course, he was not elected, but during the election campaign he had an opportunity to discuss grievances and injustices done to his people.

Unfortunately, Joseph Smith as mayor of Nauvoo and as the highest official in city government, gave the order to shut down the antagonistic newspaper "Nauvoo Expositor". At the climax of the political battle he ordered the destruction of the opposition's printing press on June 10, 1844. This unwise move was immediately vociferously denounced by his enemies as a provocative attack on freedom of the press. They demanded immediate retribution. A warrant was issued for his arrest, and Joseph Smith, his brother Hyrum and Apostle John Taylor surrendered themselves voluntarily for trial to the infamous Carthage Jail in Illinois. Joseph knew that he was led like a lamb to slaughter, and for him his last days were like running the gauntlet to his death. From prison he wrote a last letter to his beloved wife, Emma.

On July 27, 1844 Joseph Smith and his brother Hyrum were brutally murdered by a mob that stormed the prison. John Taylor was seriously wounded. Joseph tried to defend himself with a revolver which had been smuggled into the prison. He wounded three of his attackers. In 1845 all accused persons went free. The brothers Smith were buried in unmarked graves, but in 1928 their bodies were transferred to a burial site in Nauvoo.

As a god fearing lay theologian, Joseph Smith succeeded in nine short years of church activity to lead his followers from a hopeless, dormant religious faith into a vibrant religion based on divine revelation. To express it more succinctly, he replaced dry English theology with his American alternative of theophany. In an environment of persecution and expulsion, gifted men can grow into

Saints[54] and temporarily be called "prophets" and even "gods". It had been daring, of course, to call non-Mormons gentiles. When a human community is lifted up by inspired leadership and strives mightily to become more like god and live in His image, it will likely be misunderstood by outsiders and condemned. Almost without fail, the leader of such a community is perceived guilty of hubris, and plunged by hatred from his lofty heights, just like the classical "Parabata vinctus".[55] All that has little to do with the *Zeitgeist* of a single century, for even the leaders of the enlightenment movement were once falsely castigated as members of a sect and as intellectual revolutionaries. So also it was with the founder Joseph Smith and his Church. One of his important accomplishments was his ability to gather around him men of extraordinary capabilities who were able to take hold of the ensign and pass it on. The one most qualified was Brigham Young.

4.2 Brigham Young, the Second President

In the 126th revelation in the Doctrine and Covenants which Joseph Smith received on July 9, 1841, he commanded his servant and "well-beloved brother" Brigham Young, no longer to work for the conversion of people in England and Canada but "to take special care of your family from this time, henceforth and forever". This admonishment was given to a husband and father who had six children born in two marriages.[56] In ten years he had rendered unprecedented service in the Church and steadily moved up in the church hierarchy. For a year and a half he had thoroughly studied the Book of Mormon and was baptized into the Church in 1831. A year later he was ordained an elder and served twice successfully as a missionary in Canada. In 1835 he was ordained an apostle and

[54]Pseudo-Dionysius Areopagita reports such instances in his *Die Beiden Hierarchien*, ed. Joseph Stiglmayer (1911), chapter XIII § 3. Consult: Psalms 82:6.

[55]See 3.3 above.

[56]His first wife, Miriam had died of tuberculosis in 1832. In 1834 he married Ann Angel[l], "Mother Young", who survived him by five years.

helped to build the Kirtland Temple.[57] He organized the successful mission to New York and Massachusetts, evacuated the Saints in 1838 from Missouri to Illinois, skillfully planned and completed a mission to England 1838-39, and was chosen president of the Quorum of the Twelve Apostles in April 1840. The revelation in the 126th section singled him out and honored him. His organizational talent was needed, from now on, in the center of the Church. "Brother Brigham", as he was lovingly called, proceeded in all matters methodically and after having given them careful and prayerful consideration. For that reason he was much sought after in times of crisis.

What kind of a person was Joseph Smith's successor and where did he come from? Considerable research has been dedicated to that question and much has been written about it. Leonard J. Arrington's biography is generally accepted as the most definitive and in-depth work on Brigham Young. Thus I believe it will suffice if I add but a few additional remarks to round out the picture we have of him. I must admit, in the beginning of my research I had rather strange feelings when I encountered designations like "Yankee Mohammed" or "American Moses". Such embellishments give to a work the tone of a thriller which it does not deserve. This kind of grandstanding was not at all characteristic of Brigham Young. He had no need for self aggrandizement on the stage of the Latter-day Saints. He did not seek for glory; church offices, even the highest one, were offered to him because he was a hard worker, was highly qualified and needed.

Brigham Young was born on June 1, 1801 in Whitingham, Vermont as the ninth child (the fourth son) of John Young (1763-1839) and his wife Abigail "Nabby" Howe (1766-1815) from upstate New York. Brigham's father, a farmer, was a Methodist. Like the Smiths he came from a line of old New Englanders, but unlike the Smith family not all

---

[57]He was a skilled carpenter, artistic cabinet maker and glazier by profession.

his ancestors were of Anglo-Saxon descent. One can hardly imagine that Joseph Smith, Sr., would have carried a canon ball one hundred miles home as John Young did after his release from the army. Brigham's grandfather, Joseph Young, an army surgeon, married Betsy Hayden Treadway. When he died at a relatively young age she raised the six children by herself. On the maternal side the Howes' grandmother had the last name Brigham. It might be advantageous attempting to discover if the great grandfather of Joseph Young was Jacob Junge, the royal Swedish clerk who received a patent in 1654 and who served under the fourth governor of New Sweden in Fort Christina.[58] In that same year Queen Christina abdicated in favor of her cousin Karl Gustav, Duke of Pfalz-Zweibrücken.

Brigham knew only a few of his ancestors. His mother died of tuberculosis when he was fourteen years old and consequently older brothers and sisters took care of him. When he was seventeen, his authoritative father who had remarried, had him learn a trade. At first he learned to make chairs and cabinets, then he became a carpenter's apprentice, painter and glazier. He painted and helped build boats on the Erie Canal. He had an excellent reputation as a dependable worker and friend of children. When he was twenty-three he borrowed a horse and buggy, rented a house and on October 5, 1824 married Miriam Works (1806-1831), the beautiful, blond, blue-eyed daughter of Asa and Jerusha Works of Aurelia, Cayuga County, New York. The couple joined the Methodist church. Their first child, Elizabeth, was born in September 1825. Between 1827 and 1828 the Youngs moved to Oswego on Lake Ontario and a little later to Mendon in New York State where Brigham Young built a house for his family. One has to picture Brigham Young as a good-looking man, well built, five foot eight tall, short-legged, strong, with broad shoulders and energetic features who was restrained but who

---

[58]S. Donald Virdin, *Maryland and Delaware Genealogies*, 1993ff. Thomas Campania, *Nye Sverige uti America* (Stockholm, 1792). Amanda Johnson, *The Swedish Settlements on the Delaware*, 2 vols. (New York, 1911).

radiated warmth and inspired confidence. He had a large head, long wavy brown hair and steely grey eyes.[59] In Mendon, Heber C. Kimball, a blacksmith and potter by profession, born the same year as Brigham, became his life long friend. Brigham's second daughter, born in 1830, was named Vilate after her mother who was confined to a chair after her daughter's birth and died of tuberculosis two years later. Like Joseph Smith, Brigham Young was familiar with poverty in his youth and did not receive much formal education either. He himself was spared serious illness and crippling disease, but suffered the loss of close family members and relatives.

As a human being, a Christian, family man, missionary, and apostle, Brigham Young, a man acquainted with sorrow, was prepared in the summer of 1844 to master the crisis which occurred for the Church of Jesus Christ of Latter-day Saints upon the death of their prophet Joseph Smith. On August 8, 1844, thousands of Latter-day Saints assembled in a wooded area next to the Mississippi River to attend a meeting called hastily by Sidney Rigdon, the ambitious and former close associate of Joseph Smith. Before the apostles could return from their field of labor in the East, he intended to have the assembly confirm him as the prophet's successor. On previous occasions his exceptional oratorical proficiency had never failed him. He was well read in English literature, better than any other member of the Church, knew some Latin, Greek and perhaps a little Hebrew, and although he had the habit of sometimes deviating a bit off the subject, he would always return to it and made his main points. This time he failed. He did not know that Brigham Young had returned two days before and stood unrecognized off to one side. Rigdon went on and on for an hour and a half standing with his back to the wind on a heightened platform.

When Rigdon had ended, the President of the Quorum of Twelve Apostles stood up in the back of the crowd so that all had to quickly

---

[59]Werner, 182, 453-454. Arrington, 406.

turn around to see him. He surprised them with his presence and addressed them briefly. It is reported that many of those who were present, thought they actually heard the voice of the prophet Joseph.[60] The assembly had to decide that very afternoon if Rigdon was to be the prophet's successor or if the twelve apostles under Brigham's leadership were to guide the Church. There was no doubt as to the outcome. Rigdon's consuming ambition had "watered down" his usual seriousness while in this situation Young's unassuming modesty, the very effective *captatio benevolentiae,* had solidified his position. The assembled conference sustained him and the Quorum of the Twelve practically unanimously in the new leadership of the Church. Carried by the collective confidence of the Saints,[61] Brigham Young, as God's chosen vessel, completed the construction of the Nauvoo Temple and prepared himself spiritually through fervent prayer to lead the great trek to the West, about which we wrote in 2.2 above.

During the exodus, on January 14, 1847 at Winter Quarters on the West Bank of the Missouri River, the uncontested leader announced his only revelation included in the Doctrine and Covenants.[62] In this unique report, the Lord's steward gives detailed instructions for the trek and prepares the Saints for "the glory of Zion". About Joseph Smith's martyrdom he writes, "it was needful that he should seal his testimony with his blood, that he might be honored and the wicked might be condemned".[63] Fate had taken its course.

---

[60]Werner stresses on p. 190 that Young seemed to have actually been transformed physically into Joseph's likeness and that Joseph had "loaned" him his voice. Arrington reports the meeting on p. 115, and says that Young had a powerful voice, 406.

[61]At the end of August, Brigham's position was further strengthened when he was appointed Lieutenant General of the Nauvoo Legion.

[62]D&C 136.

[63]D&C 27, 31, 39.

During the exodus to the promised land of "Deseret" a fresh well had to be dug every day, since the river water (like that of the Platte River, for example) was unsuitable for drinking. These newly dug wells contained fresh groundwater, a simile for the blessings of the new religion which daily prepared the souls of the believers for immortality.

When the pioneers had reached the Salt Lake Valley, each family received a certain plot of land, but single men and unmarried women received no land at all.[64] On the very first full day in the valley the "colonizer president" laid down the law. No one was allowed to sell his land for profit. Everybody must be industrious. Brigham Young was frequently asked, "Are you a prophet?" His answer shows his sense of humor: "I am of profit to my people."

Brigham Young had obtained a high degree in the Masonic Order, but in 1845 he disassociated himself from the organization.[65] Together with Heber Kimball and Willard Richard he had received the ordinance of washing, anointing and endowment by the prophet Joseph Smith before his death. Their children also were sealed to them, and they in turn were sealed to their parents. After Brigham had pondered for weeks the difficult and momentous question of polygyny and initially rejected it, he finally consented to the inevitability. He received permission from his wife Mary Ann, and in June 1842 married his first plural wife. Before he settled in Salt Lake City he had married an additional ten wives who in the course of time bore him forty-eight children. Some of these died in infancy. Another six wives remained childless.[66] In 1847 he had twelve families and

---

[64]Arrington, 168.

[65]Arrington, 452, endnote 7. John A. Widtsoe, *Joseph Smith*, chapter 49.

[66]Arrington, Appendix C. Two wives who had no children divorced him, one in 1851 and one in 1876. Initially he had married Miriam Works who died and then Mary Ann Angell. He had twenty-seven plural wives and a total of fifty-seven children [fifty-six according to Werner]. Forty reached adulthood, some a ripe old age, on average 63 years.. Seven wives presented him with more than one child.

was eligible to receive twelve pieces of land – or eight if only wives with children were counted. Arrington[67] reports that each parcel of land was one and one-quarter acres large and that Brigham Young chose ten acres east of Temple Square for himself and his eight wives who had children,[68] which shows that he obeyed the rules of land distribution. Such a detail provides us with an important insight into his character and explains why the Saints completely trusted him.

"Mother" Mary Ann Young and her children lived in the White House or Mansion House which no longer exists. Ann Decker Seeley Young lived in the "Beehive House",[69] and was in charge of the entire household. This was the official residence of the president who spent the last twenty years of his life in it. In 1855 the famous "Lion House", an impressive three- story splendid edifice, was completed. At times twelve families lived in it. It also served as a school for the Young children. These buildings, a small water mill and stables were fenced in by an eight foot high wall.

Brigham Young's settlement policy was closely connected with his missionary policy. During his lifetime he established about five hundred Mormon communities,[70] some as far away as California, Idaho and Arizona. To aid the settlers financially the Perpetual

---

Only three of his plural wives died before Brigham. The average age of his wives was 65 years. Brigham Young died when he was 76. Arrington states that some thirty women were "sealed" to Brigham "for eternity" only, and that he did not share their earthly life.

[67]Arrington, 168. See also *The Essential Brigham Young (*Salt Lake City, 1992).

[68]Arrington, 171 for farm land and additional city lots purchased later.

[69]I visited this solidly constructed and aesthetically pleasing house several times in 1977 and 1998.

[70]Arrington, 172. See also his *Great Basin Kingdom: An Economic History of the Latter-day Saints* (1958 and 1966).

Emigrating Fund Company[71] was founded. It set conditions for more equitable payments and repayments.

Starting in the 1850s President Young began establishing four kinds of colonies:

1. permanent settlements for new immigrants in the Salt Lake Valley,
2. production centers for iron, coal, cotton, flax, molasses, and other resources,
3. temporary camps for the resettlement of pioneers,
4. stations for various Indian Missions.[72]

Tithing both in cash and kind was the essential financial resource. It was paid by the head of every LDS family. Much internal billing was handled via the bartering system.

Since the Salt Lake Temple would not be completed for many years to come, many spiritual and secular matters were taken care of in the Old Tabernacle or in the Endowment House. Brigham's major responsibilities were the organization of wards, the calling of bishops, the appointment and preparation of new apostles, and the selection of capable and trusted advisors and counselors. Counselors in the First Presidency were Heber Kimball who functioned so to speak as registrar, and Willard Richards who also was the first editor of the "Deseret News" which is still Salt Lake City's daily newspaper. Jedediah Grant succeeded him as editor and became mayor of the city. Daniel Wells was the next mayor and was also appointed lieutenant general of the Nauvoo Legion. George A. Smith, the cousin of Joseph Smith, was Church Historian.

---

[71] It was founded in 1849 and freed potential immigrants from dependency on immigration agents in Europe and the United States.

[72] Arrington, 174-175.

> As a public figure, Brigham Young was a mixture of idealism and pragmatism. The idealistic path of service to his people intertwined with the pragmatic goal of preserving his status, power, and influence.[73]

He was not a systematic theologian, but rather a pragmatic thinker. Under his supervision, others were given responsibility of making sure that church teachings passed the test of orthodoxy and that doctrinal understanding remained sound. He would not tolerate incorrect limitations imposed upon him for "all creation is in progress".[74] For this reason he was able to reach the following surprisingly bold conclusion: "Mormonism embraces all truth that is revealed and that is unrevealed, whether religious, political, scientific, or philosophical."[75]

Experts, like Arrington, who read President Young's 800 preserved sermons, are of the opinion that he felt it was the duty of every living person to steadily keep on progressing like Adam and Eve, and in this sense to cultivate and populate the earth: "Man is a God in embryo, with a capacity of endless growth, development, and joy."[76]

In 1849 there was still hope that the U.S. Congress would recognize the Mormon State of Deseret. This state would have included today's Utah, the Colorado River Valley to the Gila River in Arizona, southeastern Idaho, southwestern Wyoming, western Colorado, New Mexico, northern Arizona, southeastern California,[77] and southeastern Oregon, an area twice as large as the Federal Republic of Germany. Although after two years the dream was shattered, when statehood was denied, these two years were used effectively. The State University

---

[73]Arrington, 200.

[74]Arrington, 203. Journal of Discourses 1:350 cited by Arrington.

[75]Arrington, 204. JD 9:14 cited by Arrington.

[76]Arrington, 205. JD 7:286 cited by Arrington.

[77]As far as the seaport of San Diego situated on the Pacific Ocean.

of Deseret[78] was created, and the Church of Jesus Christ of Latter-day Saints with its carefully developed structure was officially incorporated.

In September 1850 U.S. President Fillmore appointed Brigham Young Governor of the Utah Territory and combined his governorship with the responsibility as Superintendent for Indian Affairs. The reason for this appointment may have been to limit the territorial governor's general political influence by diverting his responsibilities to Indian matters. The reduced territory encompassed 188,000 square miles, the size of Spain today. Today the State of Utah with 85,000 square miles is the eleventh largest state of the union.

When General Robert E. Lee surrendered the army of the Confederate States, and consequently slavery was abolished , Brigham Young feared that the Federal Government would renew its strict control of polygyny in Utah and that federal troops would be sent to Salt Lake City and Utah.

The economic competition between Mormon and non-Mormon enterprises was especially fierce. The founding of Zion's Cooperative Mercantile Institution (ZCMI) turned out to be a clever chess move. It quickly became profitable and soon distributed considerable dividends to its owners.

Shortly before Young's death, several of his sons were enrolled as students in distinguished American universities: the US Military Academy at West Point in New York State, the University of Michigan in Ann Arbor, the Rensselaer Polytechnical Institute in Troy (New York State), and the U.S. Naval Academy in Annapolis, Maryland. In 1875 the Brigham Young Academy[79] was established in Provo, Utah

---

[78]Today the University of Utah, founded 1850. See below 5.2.

[79]Today, with more than 30,000 students, the renowned Brigham Young University is the largest private university in the United States.

and the Brigham Young College in Logan. "It is clear that Brigham's dream of establishing a homogeneous cooperative community did not come to fruition."[80] Nevertheless, under the prevailing circumstances he came as close as was humanly possible.

In summary, our judgment of Brigham Young's accomplishment as one of the founding fathers of the church is as follows: he did not only complete the hierarchic church structure during the early period, and it persists to this day,[81] but he was also responsible for the cooperative economic success of the area. He introduced a well-rounded concept of man[82] (which has not been accepted without contradiction by outsiders) that is accepted by the LDS individual and the community at large. His message is: man, favored with considerable attention from above, finds himself in a state of transition between life and death, between renewal and dying, a state that is constantly renewed. Baptism, marriage and other selected sacred ordinances have a guardian or protective function. Plural marriage does not minimize secular or temple marriage. Through the ordinance of baptism for the dead, deceased ancestors take part in life directly because the hereafter is considered to be spiritually alive, not dead. The temple sealing ordinance summarizes the seriousness of life symbolically, and the veil of sacredness must not be removed from it so that promised blessings will not be withheld.

The Mormon philosophy which Brigham Young bequeathed his priesthood leaders and his faithful followers, represents a covenant between a planned form of life, natural resources intelligently developed by man's activity, and divine blessings hoped for. Without these, a Christian religion can not survive.

---

[80]Arrington, 381. The universities, however, became very successful.
[81]Arrington, 402-404.
[82]With respectful caution one could perhaps call it theosophy.

4.3 John Taylor, the Third President

John Taylor was called to the Quorum of the Twelve Apostles in 1838. As apostle and confidant of the President of the Church he accompanied Joseph Smith and Hyrum Smith in 1844 to the Carthage Jail. During the attack he was severely wounded, but later recovered. Brigham Young, Heber Kimball, and the Pratt brothers respected him very much. He was asked to write the eulogy for the prophet and his brother.[83]

Taylor was born in England in 1808. He attended school for several years and received a good education. When he was 24 years old he and his parents emigrated to Canada. He became a Methodist minister. In 1836 both he and his wife joined the Mormon Church. On account of his fluent writing style he was appointed publisher of the Nauvoo newspaper "Times and Seasons".

Together with Brigham Young and Orson Pratt he fulfilled an extended mission in England. After his return in the fall of 1846, he and Parley Pratt led a large party of about 1500 Saints across the plains to the Salt Lake Basin. Brigham Young then sent him on a mission to France and Germany. During his sojourn in Europe in 1852 he wrote and published in Liverpool a basic reference work on the Church, entitled *The Government of God*.[84]

When he had returned to Salt Lake City he was elected a member of the legislative council, 1852-1855. Later he was appointed President of the American Eastern States Mission and published the church publications *The Mormon* and in France *Etoile du Deseret.* Back home with his family which by now consisted of seven wives and

---

[83]D&C 135.

[84]For biographic information on John Taylor consult Samuel W. Taylor, *The Kingdom or Nothing; The Life of John Taylor, Militant Mormon* (New York, 1976). The main title was Taylor's personal motto. Repr. *The Last Pioneer* (Salt Lake City, 1999).

thirty-five children,[85] he was elected to the legislature, became speaker of the Utah House of Representatives,[86] judge in Utah County and for a time Superintendent of Education for the State of Utah.

In Arras, France, Apostle Taylor had inspected a sugar beet factory and sent a technical report to Brigham Young. As a consequence, expensive machinery was imported to Utah, and the Deseret Manufacturing Company for the production of sugar was established. It turned out to be a substantial failure, and the Church lost at least $50,000. Taylor was more successful with the founding of wool manufacture and iron production.[87]

Taylor was a good-looking man, tall, and had a "magnetic figure with slightly grey hair". He was a skilled orator and defender of Mormonism in word and script. In 1869 Taylor got into a heated debate with the U.S. Vice President Schuyler Colfax who had visited Utah and published an article in the "New York Times" in which Taylor argued that plural marriage had been instituted by God and could therefore not somehow be eliminated by the laws of man. Taylor won the debate and when he returned to Utah this masterful Mormon writer and defender of the faith was celebrated as the "lion of the entire valley". He was not a personal close friend of Brigham Young – their personalities were too different – but the aging president realized that he would be his most capable successor. Both Orson Hyde and Orson Pratt, because of differences, had left the Church for a year and therefore lost their seniority in the Quorum of Twelve Apostles, and President Young reminded the quorum who, according to the order of the Church, was the senior apostle and who therefore was in line for the presidency. On September 4, 1877 Taylor had become President of the Quorum of the Twelve. In 1880, the year in which the Pearl of Great Price was officially accepted as a

---

[85]D. Bitton, *Dictionary*, 239-240.
[86]Arrington, 374-376.
[87]Arrington, 184-187.

standard work of the Church, he became President of the Church until he died in 1887. On September 5 and 6, in his first year in office, U.S. Vice President Rutherford Hayes and his advisors visited Utah, but no accommodation was reached.

Taylor's period in office is characterized by the preservation of the many accomplishments. The Edmunds Act exhorted strong pressure on Church leaders finally to give way in the controversy about polygyny. To avoid persecution and incarceration President Taylor had to go into hiding and to live under an assumed name. During his time as president it became clear that the Utah territory would not become a state until the conditions for attaining statehood had been finalized. Utah had the requisites for statehood, but lacked support for it in Washington.

The settlement of the late Brigham Young's considerable estate was challenging. Church property had to be divided from personal property. The family received their holdings in the Deseret National Bank, the Utah Northern, Southern and Western Railroads, the Woollen Mill in Provo and their stock in ZCMI. Public buildings, ZCMI, several factories, and other valuables went to the Church. John Taylor distinguished himself in helping to settle this difficult matter.[88] The procedure of apostolic succession which had been instituted by Brigham Young, survived the pressure brought to bear by Young's two oldest sons from his marriage with Mary Ann Angell, Brigham, Jr., (1836-1903) and John W. Young (1844-1924). However, "Prince John", as Brigham had once called John Taylor, held the reigns of leadership tightly in his hands.[89] Just like Brigham Young had once warded off the pretensions in favor of her sons by Joseph Smith's widow Emma[90], so John Taylor now succeeded in leading the Church, embedded in family ties, on the path of rightful succession.

---

[88]Arrington, appendix D.

[89]Arrington, 198.

[90]In 1846 she married the non-Mormon Lewis C. Bidamon, managed a boarding house and died in 1879.

Ever since Joseph Smith's death, Church leadership had always reverted to the Quorum of Twelve Apostles which is equal in authority to the First presidency, and the President of the Quorum has succeeded the President of the Church. Such is the order of the Church.[91]

4.4 Assessment of the Essential Accomplishments During the Founding Phase

I consider the new concept of man existing in a transformed environment to be the most important achievement of the leadership of the Church during the founding years. This is apparent everywhere in a new (but at the same time old) conduct of life which has led with the help of education to a secure faith among the Mormon people.

A Mormon, growing up in the 20th and 21st centuries, makes voluntary decisions about his faith. His baptism at age eight takes place while he is standing, i.e. not as an infant when he can not yet speak or think for himself. Responsibilities are not dispensed catechetically but are gradually put to the test until they are spiritually absorbed.

As early as 1870, women in Utah were given the right to vote and encouraged to share in making political decisions. This must have had a beneficial effect on the pedagogical climate of Mormon families from 1900 on.

Again and again, every generation of young Mormon men submit to a special kind of discipline which is essential if they are to endure the two year absence from their homes while serving as missionaries, without suffering psychological damage Since always two young missionaries serve together in bringing souls into the kingdom, they are relatively protected from possible danger.

---

[91]D&C 107:23-24.

The basic model of group life at home is apparently compensated by the mission "adventure" which is registered on the gauge of experience. Another result of the efforts during the founding years is constantly replenished self-renewal. This probably can not be done much differently by modern men than our first and founding parents, Adam and Eve, did it, when they had to decide between the tree of life and the tree of knowledge. Every man must make this choice anew.

The Bible and the Book of Mormon are two beacons for the basic orientation of the faithful. The acceptance of the latter can be compared to the New Testament prevailing against the Torah which in turn was influenced by new concepts of faith.

The anchoring of extraordinary men in the Quorum of the Twelve Apostles can be compared to the College of Cardinals in the Catholic Church. However, the successor to the president in the Church of Jesus Christ of Latter-day Saints is not chosen like the pope is in the Catholic Church, rather he is called from and sustained by a reservoir of talented candidates. Like an officer on the general staff he must prove his ability in the planning room before he can give orders that are to be obeyed in the field.

The manner of proclaiming new doctrine by revelation has been practiced very rarely since the death of Joseph Smith. That alone proves consolidation. The extraordinary accomplishments by the first six presidents during the founding years can be summarized very briefly as follows:

President Smith — Spiritual Leadership

The conversion of "sacred" knowledge contained in the Book of Mormon into a powerful living church command structure occurs in a kind of spiritual temple rededication. The prophet's martyrdom propels the future expansion of the Church of Jesus Christ of Latter-day Saints in an ever expanding direction.

President Young — Pragmatism

The metamorphosis of the spiritual church structure referred to above happens gradually in a dedicated homeland, the "New Zion", which is visible to everyone in the Salt Lake Basin settlements. The reduction of Deseret to Utah at the same time produces a society which no longer poses a danger to the existence of a Mormon community.

President Taylor — Rigorism

The firm position of the church leadership either to stoutly defend the "kingdom" or to witness its destruction leads to renewed persecution and legal restrictions as it did with the early Christians. Finally the compromise with the power of the state — as in the case of Byzantine Christianity — led to a solution.

President Woodruff — Art of Adaptation

The completion of the Salt Lake Temple in 1893, the fourth in a row, ensures the blending of the spiritual and secular strain. By abandoning the concept of polygyny, plural marriages are no longer solemnized, and the inhabitants of Utah become part of the American community which is civically organized and based on the separation of church and state.

President Snow — Worldliness

He has an excellent knowledge of human nature, a college education and is generally open minded to the world. He restores the payment of tithing which had been neglected, and tithing becomes the financial pillar of the Mormon community. The endangered financial condition of the Church is cured.

President Joseph F. Smith — Authority

Joseph F. Smith (1838-1918) was the last president who, from his childhood, could vaguely remember the Church's founder. He served as general authority of the LDS Church for over fifty years and as its president seventeen years. He had the longest beard, was strong on principles, radiated goodness and exuded firmness, became a spiritual beacon for members of the Church, and strengthened devotion to the King James version of the Bible.

One could be of the opinion, and accordingly summarize, that Presidents Smith and Taylor belonged to one group of human beings, Presidents Young and Woodruff to another. Presidents Snow and J. F. Smith could be regarded as men of the world in between the two other groups. By the way, President Woodruff[92] assumed the presidency of the Quorum of the Twelve when he was eighty years old, having been active as an apostle for fifty years. In 1889 he became President of the Church and worked in that office for nine years. When he died in 1898 he was succeeded by the eighty-six year old Lorenzo Snow (1814-1901) who had been converted in 1836. For half a century he was engaged in missionary work in England, the United States, Italy, Switzerland, Hawaii, Japan, and on the Isle of Malta. For almost thirty years he was a member of the territorial legislature and helped develop Brigham City, Utah.[93] I trust that I have covered the major aspects of the founding phases of the Church and not left out important details.

---

[92]Woodruff came from Connecticut, had nine wives and thirty-three children. Bitton, 264-65.

[93]Bitton, 225-26. J. L. Arrington, ed. *The Presidents of the Church: ... biographical essays* (Salt Lake City, 1986/93).

4.5 The Attainment of Normal Conditions. Persisting Opposition

Around 1890 the situation for the Church reached a degree of normalcy. The members did not need to fear any longer murder, persecution, or legal maneuvers outlawing the Church. The Saints were still not completely free to live their religion as they pleased, but they could safely go to work during the week and to church on Sunday. Sunday School had been organized for all ages before 1890 and functioned without problems. The Young Ladies Mutual Improvement Association began to assume responsibility for the spiritual, social and cultural welfare of fourteen year and older young ladies. The Young Men's Mutual Improvement Association had begun to serve young men in like manner, and the Primary Association taught religion to children.

Local organizations met regularly in the tabernacle. The administration of wards and stakes had been improved. Bishops had improved relations with their parish. The Church had succeeded to change from an economy relying mainly on barter to one based on currency. Priesthood quorums were given more authority by Church headquarters and thus became stronger. The Church assumed administrative responsibilities, and superimposed on that were concomitant spiritual responsibilities. By the turn of the century in 1900 the Church had more than 200,000 members.

After the death of President Lorenzo Snow, the leadership of the Church was restructured. Suffice it to say that Joseph F. Smith (1838-1918) referred to as "Fielding", was the son of the murdered Hyrum Smith, but belonged to a different generation than his predecessors.[94] He had been born into the Church and was called by Brigham Young to be an apostle when he was only twenty-seven years old. He was

---

[94]He was still a polygynist, however, and had six wives and forty-three children. Bitton, 220-222.

sixty-four when he assumed the presidency in 1901 and served in that office for seventeen years.

In 1903 a conference on the Book of Mormon was convened which standardized pronunciation of terminology, grammar and the paraphrasing of certain lines.[95] Since the legal status of the Church had not yet been finally secured – because complete separation of church and state had not been fully realized – again problems with President's Snow's family about his inheritance were encountered. During the First World War the number of missionaries was drastically reduced, but in the 1920s the work again increased and more than a thousand young men were called on a mission. During the first decade of the 20th century, the Church of Jesus Christ of Latter-day Saints gained increased respectability.[96]

At this point I wish briefly to once again touch on the turning points of LDS church history discussed above in chapter 3. The way of looking at things from the viewpoint of the main stream of reformed theology has narrowed and thus focused. In order to differentiate itself from so-called sects it concentrates its attacks particularly on Mormonism. Not until the last generation of scholars, has LDS church history become an academic discipline. Unfortunately not much of this scholarship has become known in Germany, or for that matter in Europe. The study of American economic and social history has been greatly neglected in Germany academia. The University of Münster, for example, orders almost no books in this area. R. R. Bowker, on the other hand, in the most recent collection, lists more than 300 titles about the Mormon Church,[97] but only very few specialists are familiar with this collection, which, by the way, also contains listings about the Reorganized Church.

---

[95]Thomas G. Alexander, *Mormonism in Transition, 1880-1930* (University of Illinois Press, 1986), 94-99, 303-304.

[96]Alexander, 305.

[97]*Books in Print 1997-98*, vol. 3 and 4 subject guide (New Providence, 1997).

The Reorganized Church of Jesus Christ of Latter-day Saints broke off from the main Church. After the death of Joseph Smith a controversy arose about who should be the successor of the prophet. Emma, Joseph's widow, thought that the church presidency should be hereditary and remain in the Smith family. She wanted to have her minor son, Joseph Smith III, appointed as a sort of governor of the Church until he would become of age. This proposition gained some support because of doctrinal disagreement. Emma was strictly opposed to polygyny and prevailed upon others around her to remain steadfast in their opposition. Her circle of friends did not only firmly reject polygyny but denied that Joseph Smith had ever practiced it. Besides that, this group of people had no intention to leave Illinois for an unknown destiny in the West.

Thus, Joseph Smith III, a farmer by profession, remained in Nauvoo, Illinois, got married and in 1860, when he was twenty-eight years old, was named President of the new Reorganized Church of Jesus Christ of Latter-day Saints. He moved to Iowa and founded a college. After Brigham Young's death he took courage, came to Utah in 1879 and debated the question which church had the truth. He lost the debate. When he died in 1914 his son, grandson, and great grandson succeeded him in the presidency until 1958. In 1921 the church had moved to Independence, Missouri, the former Zion. Today the Reorganized Church has about 250,000 members[98] in six hundred parishes.[99] Membership is said to be on the decline.

---

[98]Dean Jessee, *The Papers of Joseph Smith*, vol. 1, 1989, 514-515. Arrington, 118-119. Introvigne, 19-21, 174, 186. Roger Launius, *Joseph Smith III: Pragmatic Prophet* (Urbana, 1988). Steven L. Shields, *Latter-day Saint Beliefs, A Comparison between the RCJCLDS and the CJCLDS* (Independence, 1986). Douglas J. Davies ed., *Mormon Identities in Transition* (Cassell, 1996). Donald J. Breckon, *Discovering the Christ* (Herald House, 1994).

[99]O Eggenberger, *RGG*, 3rd ed. vol. IV (Tübingen, 1960), column 1141.

Opposition to the Church of Jesus Christ of Latter-day Saints has changed, as the Church itself changed and grew. It is frequently referred to as a sect which is to suggest that it has turned away from "true" Christianity. Early in the 20th century the attacks were concentrated on Joseph Smith's educational background, his so-called ignorance of the Egyptian and Hebrew languages and of theology. In the meantime his published work satisfies technical standards as it has been defended by competent scholars. It has also been critically reappraised from the standpoint of church history, at least in America. Now the success of the Church is criticized as being of dubious historical value. By the way, all modern Protestant churches carry on the work of conversion in non-Christian nations often under multi-cultural conditions. Until the 19th century, missionary centers aided German Protestants to immigrate to America.

Interest in religious literature and offers for guidance have greatly increased in the present generation. This has been enhanced by Umberto Eco's fascinating Templer novels which have prepared the climate for a pseudo non-fiction book like Wilton Barnardt's Gospel.[100] The acceptance of the musical "Jesus Christ Superstar" played a certain role.

It may not be a long time in coming until the growing acceptance of the Church will lend itself to borrowings in the techniques and the style of highly successful proselyting. The Church of Jesus Christ of Latter-day Saints will not be deceived into relaxation by its own non-vigilance. Its watchfulness will survive unexpected attack. The Church can not afford to relent from its self-critical search for the truth of its Christian religion.

---

[100] *The Thirteenth Apostle*, 1993.

5. A Comparison between Reformed Christianity and Christian Mormonism

I trust that I have demonstrated how the Mormon religion has distanced itself from Methodism and Presbyterianism and by virtue of revelations become a restored and a new Christian church. One could compare the Mormon creed with that of the Reformed Church, but one must point out that the ninth Article of Faith leaves open the possibility of change through additional revelation.[1] Thus many concepts in the Church of Jesus Christ of Latter-day Saints can be newly defined as they were in mainstream Protestant churches since the time of the concordance in 1580. In the heat of discussion this fact is often suppressed by theological quibbling. However, the tendency for rethinking, renewal and reformulating change is quite prevalent in the Mormon Church.

In all fairness, the question could be raised if Mormonism, as a Christian religion, consists of many ecclesiastical pieces[2] which the believer can gradually acquire as a code of conduct. After these varied pieces have been acquired, they become the glue[3] which holds together the religious structure for the individual and for the entire church community. On the other hand, this method of acquisition necessitates a certain comparative catechism of behavior which I will briefly treat in 5.1 below.

The power of definition inherent in the regulations of the Doctrine and Covenants and in the Articles of Faith can be compared, to some extent, to the Catechism of Reformed Protestantism. Of course, the language is entirely different, less pleading and not as professorial in

---

[1]"We believe all that God has revealed, all that He does now reveal, and we believe that He will yet reveal many great and important things pertaining to the Kingdom of God."

[2]Mark P. Leone, *Roots of Modern Mormonism* (Harvard, 1979), VI.

[3]Thomas Alexander, *Mormonism in Transition 1890-1930*, 65.

tone. All definitions are subject to endless renewal, not in the least due to the possibility of future revelation.[4] In this way the power of definition is somewhat weakened but can more easily be adapted to the changing circumstances of life.

This idiosyncratic situation makes a comparison rather difficult, for example between the Methodist Church as an important reformed denomination and the Church of Jesus Christ of Latter-day Saints. A few examples below must suffice. They are to clarify important differences for the reader. On the left side, the permanent doctrinal burden which a reformed Christian must carry is listed. The right side intends to demonstrate that the burden of religious canon is for a Mormon easier to bear. These two columns compare the traditional with a new concept of religion and show, at least in the case of the Mormon religion, that the new way has been able to supercede the traditional. Only a partial comparison of both systems of burdening the believer is intended and possible in its brevity.

For a better comprehension of the terminology used, one might refer to the Calvinist confession as a mechanism of relief from the pressure on man's conscience. The Mormon's burden is still further "alleviated".

5.1 The Dogmatic Burden Carried by the Believer of "Strict" Calvinism [left column] Compared with the Alleviated Burden of Mormonism [right column]

Dogmatic Burden	**Alleviated Burden**
For fear to provoke his Lord God, a Calvinist will hold back	For a Mormon his understanding of God is enhanced by his belief in eternal progression

[4] Ninth Article of Faith and Leone, 9.

A personal singleness of the trinity is not supposed to be part of his faith	Mormons believe that the godhead consists of three separate individuals
The last supper is a transformed sacrament that is administered by professional clergy	In the last supper, water is administered in place of wine. Bread and water are passed to the entire congregation by lay priesthood members. The last supper does not offer forgiveness of sins but is celebrated in remembrance of Christ
Salvation depends on the sacraments	Sacred ordinances alone do not guarantee salvation
Man is forever separated from the godhead	Man strives to become like God ("man is a god in embryo"[5])
Gradation in the resurrection and a godlike nature of man is anathema	At the resurrection of the body salvation is possible, but exaltation is assured after attaining one's goal
Suffering from a burden of sins since time immemorial	The rejection of the teaching of original sin liberates man from this fear and the implied heavy burden
Sin is a continuation and a renewal of the original sin	Sin is a rebellion against divine principles even when it concerns progress
Man is primarily an individual and a member of the church only secondarily	Man acts as steward for himself and for his church

Birth pains become an institution; the fear of death overshadows man's entire life	Man has a pre-mortal and post-mortal existence and thus no fear of death
The Bible's message of salvation is definitive	The Book of Mormon contains the "fullness of salvation"[6]
Christians consider themselves to be favorites of God.	God favors both the "saints" and the jews as His covenant people
Calvinists strive personally for prestige	Mormons subordinate themselves to a person who has "charisma"

5.2 Institutions

Before my final assessment of the Mormon phenomenon, I will present for consideration a few facts about the framework of the Church. Fortunately the LDS Church has recently granted interviews to three journalists[5] and provided them with detailed information and with insight into its financial situation.[6] The LDS Church is not a profit making organization[7] but a non-profit public corporation. The management of the Church has long since outgrown its baby shoes, and since the Second World War has been very successful. Below are some of the basic facts:

[5]David van Biena, S. C. Gwynne and Richard N. Ostling.

[6]"Kingdom Come" *TIME* magazine, August 14, 1997. "The Mormon Moment", *U.S. News*, November, 13, 2000, 58-65. See also R.N. Ostling and J.K. Ostling, *Mormon America: The Power and the Promise*. N.Y. 1999.

[7]German journalists do not yet make a sufficiently clear distinction between an organization existing for profit like "Scientology" and a non-profit organization such as the LDS Church. See "*Neue Juristische Wochenschrift*", 1997, No. 13, 832ff.

Membership has steadily grown.[8] "Since the Second World War, its ranks have expanded more than 10-fold, with a worldwide membership today of over 11 million – more than half outside the United States."[9] In the USA live 5.1 million members, in South America 2.5 million, in Mexico 847,000, in Asia 711,000, in Central America 455,000, in the South Pacific 355,000, in Europe 228,000, in the UK and Ireland 176,000, in Canada 157,000, in Africa 137,000, and in the Carribean 110,000.[10]

It is assumed that the annual income from the payment of tithing (members pay one tenth of their income) worldwide amounts to $5.9 billion, from investments $600 million.[11] Judged by its financial situation, its weight and influence, the LDS Church is a very successful multinational corporation. Tithing paid worldwide by members can be called a second income tax. In 1996 $4.9 billion were sent from American church units to headquarters in Salt Lake City and an additional $300 million from outside the United States. Most of the money is used for the construction of temples and chapels,[12] Brigham Young University, other colleges and schools, missionary work, and welfare projects. The Church operates sixteen radio stations, a TV station, and in Utah thirty outlets of the Deseret Book Co.

A pair of home teachers (priesthood holders) visit each family every month and take care of the family's spiritual and other needs. Thus, in the final analysis, faith and social coherence are the basis of the

---

[8] In the United States it has a growth rate of 220% annually and has become the fifth largest religious denomination. The Roman Catholic Church is still the largest. *U.S. News,* 61.

[9] *U.S. News,* 61

[10] *U.S. News,* 61.

[11] More than $ 6 billion are invested abroad. In the United States the value of 50 farms and ranches, for example, is worth $ 5 billion. The biggest cattle ranch is the 312,000 acre Deseret Cattle & Citrus Ranch outside of Orlando in Florida.

[12] More than one hundred temples are either completed or under construction, and more than one chapel per day is completed worldwide.

Mormon's quality of life. They are also the source of the economic strength of the Church.

The Church is organized in 2,600 stakes and 650 districts consisting of 26,000 wards and branches, and 350 missions.[13] The two oldest universities in the State of Utah, the University of Utah in Salt Lake City and Brigham Young University[14] in Provo, are renowned educational institutions. On account of its prestige the University of Utah can be compared to the University of Oregon in Eugene. Brigham Young University has a beautiful campus at the foot of the magnificent Rocky Mountains and is the best endowed private university in the United Sates. Academically it can be compared to Notre Dame University in Indiana.[15] The mission of Brigham Young University is "to assist individuals in their quest for perfection and eternal life". All students are to be taught the truth of the Christian gospel, receive a broad general education, "enlarge their intellect by developing skills" and by learning modern research methods. Each must declare a major area of study.[16] After eight semesters of study the student graduates with the bachelor of arts or science degree.[17]

The mission of the University of Utah[18] is to educate the individual and to impart general knowledge. It considers itself to be the "flagship of the state's system of higher education". In 1998 more than 25,000

---

[13]2001-2002 Church Almanac (Salt Lake City, 2000), 422-424.

[14]The "Word Perfect" program was essentially developed by members of this university.

[15]"America's Best Colleges" in *U.S. News*, 1998, 73 and 72.

[16]*BYU Undergraduate Catalogue*, 2000, xiii-xv. The Board of Trustees developed the goals of education in 1981. The university has 75 academic departments that offer a so-called "major". Annual tuition amounts to approximately $ 3000 for members of the Church and more than $ 4000 for non-members. For principles of academic freedom consult the catalogue, xvii-xx.

[17]The Law School offers a law degree, and several departments the master's and doctor's degree.

[18]It is divided into 15 colleges including medicine and law.

students were enrolled compared with more than 30,000 at Brigham Young University. Tuition for Utah residents is approximately $3000.

Prejudice and misunderstanding about the Church's missionary program still exist. Every capable young men is expected to serve for two years as a missionary, but in reality only about 60%[19] or about 50,000 serve. Much fewer young women serve for eighteen months. A missionary language training school[20] is located in Provo. In 1991 the ratio of converts per missionary pair was about six a year.[21]

5.3 Summary: The Significance of Mormonism

The Mormon style of living, characterized by baptism through immersion, the laying on of hands for blessings, and communal participation in the last supper, is predominantly Christian. Their concept of time differs, however, from other denominations. Time does not only mean money, as it does for every modern American, but is a precious commodity and "ennobles" the daily life of the active Mormon Christian. As a steward of his time, he is accountable for its intelligent use, which is characterized by his willingness to serve his fellow man and by an active work ethic. In the sense that time is organized it is typically "American". Since 1833 Mormons have been commanded to live chaste, abstain from alcoholic beverages, coffee, black tea, and the use of tobacco, and to eat meat sparingly.[22] This life style is designed to promote physical health and increase spiritual awareness. It has been statistically demonstrated that the average Mormon lives longer than the average non-Mormon.

---

[19]*U.S. News,* 60.

[20]Formerly (till 1961) the "Missionary Language Institute" was located in Salt Lake City.

[21]According to information available in the Provo training school. See also Bitton, 144.

[22]D&C 89.

The temple ceremony shows an affinity to freemasonry. I believe it was instituted as a protective wall during the period of intense persecution and can be regarded as a framework and mechanism of selection.[23] More important, however: before becoming a member, a potential convert must demonstrate faith, repent of his sins, be baptized by a person who has authority, receive the Holy Ghost by the laying on of hands, and become an active member in his parish.

Mormon anthropology ideally depicts man in the image of God and the Creator as an exalted man. At this point Mormon philosophy reaches its limits which it has in common with mysticism and modern science. In 1833 the prophet Joseph Smith was told by revelation that all truth and all intelligence is independent.[24] Mormonism as a total phenomenon[25] is somewhat different, but not fundamentally so from Christianity[26] nor is it opposed to science.[27] On the contrary, although Mormonism at first glance appears a bit foreboding to the outsider, on closer scrutiny it soon emerges as a powerful pacesetter for Christianity on the way to spiritual enlightenment and as a preliminary step towards additional inspiration. The enlightenment continues to shine from America in all directions world-wide.

---

[23]Until 1984 the free masons did not accept Mormons as members. Introvigne, 130-131. See also "Freemasonry and the Temple" in *Encyclopedia of Mormonism*, vol. II, 528-529.

[24]D&C 93:30, 33.

[25]The leadership of the American Presbyterian Church until 1995 felt differently. Particularly in Utah the LDS Church is regarded heretical by the Presbyterians.

[26]David Flusser, Professor of Judaism at the Hebrew University in Jerusalem, reserves judgment in the question whether there is a separation between Mormonism and Christianity or not. "Das Schisma zwischen Judentum und Christentum," *Evangelische Theologie*, XL (1980), 214-239. Reprint in *Immanuel*, 16 (1983), 32-49.

[27]Alvin K. Benson, "Joseph Smith on Modern Science," in *Joseph Smith, the Man* (1993), Susan Black and Charles Tate eds., chapter 12, 151-167.

5.4 The Use of Language by Mormons as a Vehicle of Faith
5.4.0 Introduction to Issues of Oral Usage

As all religions have and get accustomed to a certain manner of expressing their faith, my question raised in the end is: does the Mormon language use its own "grammar", too? By "grammar" I understand a set of rules conscious or unconscious that informs one's behavior. In my context I am inquiring into the behavior of the Mormons as they communicate in their religious sphere, for example in prayer, which form of communication is particularly striking to the outside observer, perhaps even strikingly appealing. An example would be, when a Mormon is recognized by his bishop in a so-called testimony meeting, he stands in order to confess his faith in front of a group of fellow Saints "bearing testimony" to the congregation in a particular manner using particular language. Another example would be, when a Mormon is asked by his bishop to give the invocation or benediction in a church service, he walks up to the pulpit, stands in front of the microphone, often folds his arms, closes his eyes, bows his head, and utters a prayer freely from the heart, a prayer that is not memorized. In doing so he uses some language that may differ from the memorized prayer language used by a Protestant or Catholic clergyman. He addresses Heavenly Father, gives thanks for particular blessings and invokes blessings upon the proceedings of the service, the speakers, members of the congregation that may be in need or ill, and on the leadership of the ward or the Church. He closes in the name of Jesus Christ, not in the name of the Father, Son and Holy Ghost.

In contrast to the typical Mormon prayer, a Catholic believer folds his hands in front of his chest, a Lutheran interlocks his fingers in a similar situation, and both relate a prescribed text by heart or by reading aloud. The language use in each case is verbally and non-verbally communicative. While watching a Mormon prayer in a church service for the first time, it became obvious to me that Mormons, by their use of language, prefer certain gestures and words over other perhaps more expected or conventional ones. The interlocking of fingers accompanying the standard Lord's Prayer (as spoken by Lutherans, for example.) is not customary to Mormons. While getting introduced to Mormon religious and civilian customs, it occurred to me that the Saints apparently use a "different" language or a different style of language. Hence it will be my task in the following to elucidate this language use from the inside of Mormondom. If anything, such observations taught this outsider that assembled members of a religious community, such as the Latter-day Saints, can communicate as participants, by using mutually familiar phrases differently. They use individual, social, and even technical ways of talking or being spoken to. They understand each other in a "public" space. Participants communicating in a religious space, share beliefs, and expect certain stereotypical gestures to be made by everybody. They share common assumptions, but, for example during a talk in a moment of awkwardness, a tongue twister can be overcome by means other than simple grammatical correction, for example by a humorous remark. In a prayer offered in a church service, the person making an error during the prayer, continues on praying, and does not necessarily retract or expand on his potentially incomplete utterance. Instead, in view of some turning point reached, which commands a new direction of energy, he would try to overcome his embarrassment by expressing the same thought differently. Thus, effective communication is neither exclusively grammatical-behavioral in kind, nor predictable behavior by itself alone, but makes use of accepted gestures and ways of self-correction. I observed this linguistic behavior in student parishes at Brigham Young University in Provo, Utah. A serious linguistic investigation demands or calls for a scientific scaling process seen as *a* system in group action. I hope to find the tools for such an investigation of the Mormons' language usage. That is my desired goal, and I trust that I will be able to summarize these tools in the final section 5.4.7. Suffice it to say at this point that oral Mormon language is not accompanied or grounded by linguistic behavior, but is behavior couched in expressing itself.

5.4.1 Introduction to Issues of Written (Scriptural) Language Usage

Scriptural language on the other hand, as it is written down by scribes, aims in a different direction than participants'oral communication in a church service, in prayer or a sermon. The latter does not need to be preserved, but only to be understood, before it passes. The scripture, on the contrary, preserves a permanent record for two purposes. First, it addresses the faithful and tries to strengthen their faith. Second, the language of the recorded document seeks to preserve the document for posterity.[28] The desired preservation may be achieved by a storing process, or by a carefully worded translation. Both these techniques were successively used in the case of Joseph Smith, first, by finding the treasure containing the plates of Mormon, and second, by translating the Book of Mormon from its apocryphal treasure sources into revealed biblical English.

The Book of Mormon amalgamates older traditions in part "as a fusion of the Old Testament and the New Testament" and provides interpretations of single biblical passages.[29] It is nowadays, as of 1982, identified as "another Testament of Jesus Christ". Last but not least, the Book of Mormon is described as "a guide to modern Christian living," quoting from Lowell L. Bennion's caption of his book about the Book of Mormon in 1985. Thus the extended recording process ultimately turns a revelation given in 1830 into understandable terminology also by modern standards. Two purposes are achieved at the same time: God's originally phrased call is preserved and the translation of it (done for the sake of human obedience) is continually reinterpreted, or at least re-framed, by fresh insights. The "law engraven upon the plates of brass" of 1 Nephi

---

[28]Book of Mormon, 1 Nephi 3:19-21.

[29]Eugene England, ed. *The Best of Lowell Bennion. Selected Writings 1928-1988* (Salt Lake City, 1993) 83. Philip L. Barlow, *Mormons and the Bible. The Place of the Latter-day Saints in American Religion* (Oxford, 1991) 29.

4:16 expresses norms that God did not have to justify. The preservation was ordered by angels, whose command triggered the translation task of keeping an apocryphal record alive within the domain of a particular people. This record kept alive, reshapes and releases linguistic energy in dictated written form, which appears to be a rather neat process. The scriptural language of the Book of Mormon is one of divinity and humanity, engraved and "translated", abridged-recorded, and finally re-recorded. In the process Mormon's own pre-hieroglyphic language has been shelved in the background. As the First Book of Nephi makes clear, the agent of the preservation, Nephi, uses his body language, to use modern terminology and gestures, and "even every whit".[30] He also uses a helper named Laban in order to get to the royal treasury, and retrieve it for his people.

The permanently framed language needs to be executed in a particular pious fashion, by asking the people for obedience to the commandments.[31] Their adherence makes a certain linguistic striving experience universal which is well grounded in supportive, yet laterally sound structures. I will delve into them deeper in the next two sections.

5.4.2 Typological Problems of Joseph Smith's Language Usage

We need to start examining Smith's texts, containing statements about religion and its doctrine, as well as his other historical pronouncements. It would also be fair to assume that the prophet as a young man took ancient scriptures more fully as his guide than later in life, when he was a recognized and self-assured religious leader. Remarkably he understood the Holy Spirit's usage of Mormon's (non-English, and to a certain degree "foreign") language.

---

[30] (The working of his mind): 1 Nephi 4:19.

[31] 1 Nephi 22:31.

How this was possible is a mystery if one were to disregard the special seeing potency made possible by the Urim and Thummim.

Joseph Smith's revelations lead a non-believing reader to occurrences of doctrinal statements. In reading the three principal scriptures, the Book of Mormon, (1830) Doctrine and Covenants, (1835) and Pearl of Great Price (posthumously appearing 1851, becoming canonical in 1880), one notices that some expressions extend groups of phrases, e. g., "and it came to pass", other usages outreach types of expressions, e. g., "free agency". Other expressions are settled near the "fountain" of his language use, e.g. the mention of "the power of the Holy Ghost", which is defined as "the gift of God" in 1 Nephi 10:17.

It needs to be pointed out that the prophet Joseph Smith, together with Sidney Rigdon, temporarily at least, studied languages (some Egyptian, Hebrew, Greek and Latin) in 1835, and German in 1843/44, which proves that he had reached a deeper interest in linguistics, and hence in enlarging his grasp of foreign languages.[32] We do not know whether this study influenced his style. Let me also assume that during the time in which he continued to dictate to his scribes, his language expressed more experience as a recognized church leader, and thus became more pragmatic and matter of fact. In working through the Doctrine and Covenants, his own current revelations take on added urgency and, in some cases, precedence over more ancient visions flowing into the Book of Mormon. His LDS ecclesiastical pragmatism became more purposeful, the doctrinal originality more pronounced. As his confidence had grown to a higher plane, its highest expression is found in the famous King Follet funeral oration, in which he redefines the god-striving qualities of his believing Saints.

---

[32]Ehat and Cook, eds. *The Words of Joseph Smith (*1843), P 211 1; TJS 310; HC V 5:42.

The typology of Joseph Smith's scriptural language usage is hard to come by, except that a Brigham Young University expert professor performed thorough, helpful spadework collecting and publishing a ground-breaking concordance.[33] It is based on primary sources only, as listed in his introduction. He wisely omitted "Joseph Smith hearsay" from the body of these sources.

Joseph Smith was in command of less than 10.000 English words, including their derivatives, when he started to write, or roughly the vocabulary of an average American English speaker. Preponderant are not low frequency occurrences of 1- 4 letter words, but rather clusters of often occurring 5 - 8 letter words. Short single words, *unicata*, are rare, standard multi-syllabled words occur more frequently. In other words, Smith uses many statements based on his revelations or visions, formulated with generally accepted words, taken from the reservoir of the language.[34] My comparative and perhaps still casual statistical data were made by looking back at my own concordance work on Hugo Grotius's Latin dramas.[35]

In keeping with the above mentioned observations, it is not surprising that the theological choice of the main scriptural source by the Holy Spirit fell on the King James Version of the Bible, and not on any other version, as the accepted committee language of the English baroque period, which was as popular in 19th century America as in England. It is clear that a committee-steered language or "tongue", 223 years later, had to sound less innovative, but as archaic, and

---

[33]Truman G. Madsen, *Concordance of Doctrinal Statements of Joseph Smith* (Salt Lake City, 1985), first edition.

[34]John A. Widtsoe, *Joseph Smith: Seeker after Truth* (Salt Lake City, 1951), 69-70, counted under 3000 general words used "in his written publications". See also R. Gary Shapiro, *An Exhaustive Concordance of the Book of Mormon Doctrine and Covenants and Pearl of Great Price* (Salt Lake City, 1977).

[35]Christian Gellinek, *Hugo Grotius: Drama Concordance* (Camden House, 1983).

hence as reliable as in 1607. This choice called for forms like "durst", "spake", "behooveth", etc.. This process of scriptural amalgamation, rather than anachronism, continued until a cross-referenced Latter-day Saints King James Version Holy Bible with modern English notes appeared in 1979. Three years later, the Book of Mormon was labeled "Another Testament of Jesus Christ" irrespective of the enmeshment of various linguistic levels.

It might well be that the Doctrine and Covenants, written in more modern English, is a prime source of doctrine more so than the Book of Mormon, the biblical word frequency of which has been compared to both Testaments of the Bible.[36] The "Reformed-Egyptian", or better Nephitic, language of father and son, Mormon and Moroni, as alleged prime and principal source of the Book of Mormon can not yet be ascertained, since the recorded plates are unavailable, and the lost rules formerly laid down for the Saints became "unre-recordable". People living more than 2000 years apart cannot be communicative to one another, but have changed their linguistic behavior widely. All we can do in our reconstructive operation is to ascertain and describe the "behavior" of various layers of language blended by the prophet from inspired sources, with the help of the Holy Ghost, in a supernatural way. In this process of amalgamation, Joseph Smith became the communicative individual with the highest religious energy of formulating power. The revelations received linked the existing biblical language (called tongue then) of the early seventeenth century to laying the groundwork for establishing communication in modern times.

---

[36]See Philip L. Barlow, *Mormons and the Bible. The Place of the Latter-day Saints in American Religion* (Oxford, 1991) 28, footnote 41 and 42. Some 50.000 occurrences of the Book of Mormon were either borrowed from the King James Version of the Bible, or were of common usage, and many phrases of three or more words are common to both books as well. See Eldin Ricks's *Thorough Concordance of the LDS Standard Works*. F A R M S (Provo, 1995).

The scriptural language of the Mormons, perhaps surprisingly, is not meant to separate believers from the Christian religion, rather it is created to complement, rejuvenate and complete it. It added a caption, "Another Testament of Jesus Christ", enlightening people for several generations to come. The "garment" of the believing Saint is, according to 2 Nephi 1:23, supposed to be a spiritual "armor of righteousness". This believer's armor is heavier or lighter in weight for individual believers to carry. One cannot speak as an initiated participant, unless one is an active believer.

The temporary knowledge of a prophet, uttered at a particular time during the history of his church, can be gauged by its clarity, frequency or infrequency, or by its power, but not render us an objective measuring device for a permanent "meaning". Linguistically speaking, the Book of Mormon, the Doctrine and Covenants and the Pearl of Great Price do not purport different "meanings", due to their different language usage, but offer revelatory responses to various challenges. The record preserved may have been "engraven", the meaning of it cannot exactly be the same for all believers at all times. Hence, prophetic statements carry "equivalent" truth values. Various forms of transporting religious thoughts and participatory functions cannot be separated from each other. The prophetic language facility links a supernatural ingredient together. The prophetic linguistic energy is, at least partially if not preponderantly, engendered by the Spirit, which is accepted by believers to be "holy" while working its blessings.

In the case of a seer such as Joseph Smith, mindful of his other youthful activities, it is not relevant that he may have developed from an as yet not fully endowed "true prophet" to a completely designated "true prophet", when (after the forthcoming of the Book of Mormon) he picked up power and put into relief a different linguistic shape[37]

---

[37]Note the passage in the King Follet Funeral Oration: "Every man has a right to be a false prophet, as well as a true prophet"-, compiled and edited by

with the issuance of the Doctrine and Covenants. In that case, once he felt assured of his linguistic perspective, he expressed his self-chosen linguistic preferences. A truly false prophet would have stayed dependent on the rigid dogma of his and his forebears' grammar, while a prophet true to himself and his calling and in respect to his believers, would continue developing his religiously inspired resolution.

5.4.3 The "Heretical" Line of Scriptural Language Usage Extended by non-Mormons

If a religious denomination, such as the Church of Jesus Christ of Latter-day Saints, is accused of heresy from the point of view of mainstream religion, I must at the outset assume that the language used contains heretical elements, too. Accused of heresy also, but never brought to trial, was the noted American professor of divinity at Yale, Horace Bushnell (1802-1876).[38] He shared a few basic tenets both with Hugo Grotius and with Joseph Smith, in respect to their mutual understanding of truth in language, and both also shared some points of doctrine. Bushnell, in particular, thought that spiritual "facts" could only be expressed in poetical language. This seems a surprising coincidence e. g. in view of 2 Nephi 7: 4, where Nephi's brother Jacob is quoting Isaiah 50:4. Isaiah speculates about the "tongue" and the "ear" of the "learned". Furthermore, traces of Grotius's atonement theory are found in Bushnell's *The Vicarious Sacrifice*[39] "satisfying the demands of justice". For Bushnell the

---

Andrew F. Ehat and Lyndon W. Cook, *The Words of Joseph Smith: The Contemporary Accounts of the Nauvoo Discourses of the Prophet Joseph Smith.* Grandin Book Company, 341. Ronald W. Walker, "Joseph Smith. The Palmyra Seer," *BYU Studies* 24, no. 4 (1984) 461-472.

[38]Mary H. Cheney, ed., *Collected Works of Horace Bushnell*, in 11 plus 1 volumes. 1876-1881. Second edition (New York, 1903). The writer gratefully acknowledges receipt of a "Horace Bushnell scholarship" for Yale in 1961.

[39]N. Y. Scribner's 1866. See Alma 22:14. Bushnell may have known W. M. L. de Wette's *De Morte Jesu Christi expiatoria Commentatio* (Berlin, 1813).

godhead, as fountain of truth, is not only "instrumentally three" (also in respect to suffering alone) but three *and* one, "a real *quaternity* ... of persons".[40] Concomitantly there are, he discovered, two languages in every language, one being misused or abused "as great part of our religious difficulties".[41] When he contended that "the smoke of human wisdom was to stifle the breath of religion",[42] he argued along similar lines that, according to Joseph Smith also, Christianity needed to be restored, because it had fallen and degenerated from early Christianity. Joseph Smith would have agreed with the Yale professor, when the latter stated: "We can never come into a settled consent in the truth, until we better understand the nature, capacities and incapacities of language, as a vehicle of truth."[43] Horace Bushnell, as Joseph Smith, profoundly modified 19th century American protestant religion, but ironically Bushnell also, at the same time, continued Grotius's and Joseph Smith's "heretical" lines of argumentation in his chapter entitled God and Language. Smith and Bushnell, had they met, would have also agreed that the official Protestant dogmatic view, declared from many a pulpit in New England, did not inspire people to believe, while they were doing good deeds for others, and that American Christians deserved better than to see their splendid native piety suffocated, instead of stirred to action by imagination and vision. "It is hope, cherished by many of

---

John W. Rogerson, *W. M. L. de Wette Founder of Modern Biblical Criticism: An Intellectual Biography* (Sheffield, 1992), 130ff., does not realize that De Wette held "Mormon"-like positions on atonement and damnation, for which the Prussian king dismissed him in 1819 from his professorship at the University of Berlin as a "heretic" (for pseudo-political reasons).

[40]*God in Christ*. Three Discourses delivered at New Haven, Cambridge and Andover with a Preliminary Dissertation on Language (Hartford, 1849), Rp. 1972, 108-109. Textual emphasis is mine. See also De Wette, *Ueber Religion und Theologie,* 2nd ed.(Berlin, 1821), 237; *Lehrbuch der christlichen Dogmatik,* 2nd ed. (Berlin, 1818), 241; *Das Wesen des christlichen Glaubens (*Basel, 1846), § 100.

[41]*God in Christ*, 12.

[42]*God in Christ,* 287.

[43]*God in Christ* 40.

the most thoughtful and earnest Christians of our time that God is preparing the introduction at last of some new religious era."[44] He did not meet the Saints's sense of "participation and responsibility that generates the steadfast Mormon loyalty".[45]

5.4.4 Internal LDS Language Defenses after 1844

Brigham Young (1801-1877), the successor as president of the Church of Jesus Christ of Latter-day Saints, was a moving speaker of deep convictions. Many of his sermons survived through the efforts of stenographers.[46] Among several innovative church policies he discontinued his predecessor's predilection for keeping a written record of his revelations. In fact, section 136 in the Doctrine and Covenants is the only revelation that the prophet Brigham Young allowed to be included in the canon. It reads, however, like a captain's command to his crew, which was supposed "to listen together".[47] His way of adapting and shaping the Mormon language, compared to that of Joseph Smith's covenants, had moved his, and ultimately the Church's, style forward into less controversial areas. The Mormon language moved away from its baroque beginnings.

Parley P. Pratt (1807-1857), the father of modern pamphleteering, had become a right-hand man to both Joseph Smith and Brigham Young and was a member of the Council of the Twelve Apostles. His *Voice of Warning,* published in England in 1838, became my own personal introduction to reading the Book of Mormon in German translation, done by Daniel Ca(i)rn, the first German mission president. As the New Testament leaves open prophecies concerning

---

[44]*God in Christ*, 279, 345-346, 351. Bushnell admired Walt Whitman`s language.

[45]Fawn M. Brodie, *No Man Knows my History. The Life of Joseph Smith, 2nd ed.* (New York, 1945/1986), 402.

[46]Leonard Arrington, *Brigham Young: American Moses* (Chicago, 1986), 405, reports 800 sermons were recorded.

[47]Doctrine and Covenants 136:41.

the impending "end-time", the Book of Mormon, in Pratt's opinion, corrects this biblical scriptural *lacuna*. He shifts the balance from the written inter-sectional scripture to the spoken word, just as Brigham Young did in Utah.

Parley's younger brother, Orson Pratt (1811-1881), referred to as the "St. Paul of the Mormons", became the most famous and flamboyant of the twelve apostles after Brigham Young, and undoubtedly the leading Mormon pamphleteer and scriptural scholar of his time. He greatly influenced the language of the Mormons. But Orson Pratt was more than that. He also was the leading intellectual defender of Mormon language itself. He shared Joseph Smith's "literalism" with enthusiasm. Brigham Young might have argued that both the Bible and the Book of Mormon contain models of expected Saintly Christian behavior. For Orson Pratt the question was, which particular part of the scriptures selectively to imitate? He was a man of a solid scientific bent of mind and believed in correct verifiable procedures, before they were to be applied to the defense of religious language. Brigham Young superimposed his own prophetic authority on the style of his pronouncements issued by him on a day to day basis.

According to the noted biblical scholar, Philip L. Barlow,[48] the linguistic controversy between Young and Pratt may be abbreviated as follows: Pratt reconciled Mormon revelation with the Bible, Young believed in the primacy of the seer's (Joseph Smith's as well as his own) grasp of common sense issues. Apostle Orson Pratt believed "horizontally" in following scripture, the Apostle and Prophet Brigham Young "vertically" or hieratically in authentic, definitive Saintly behavior. Both men were in agreement, however, that "the bible was insufficient guide to religious life".[49] In my terminology, the

---

[48]*Mormons and the Bible (*Oxford, 1991), 92. For further background information see Nathan O. Hatch and Mark A. Noll, eds., *The Bible in America: Essays in Cultural History (* Oxford, 1981).

[49]Barlow, 88.

human language as a practical tool needed to be extended. Out of both men's ingrained respect for the English language as their mother tongue, these two New Englanders had fixed their attention on the King James Version of the Bible. Although Mormon spake rather than spoke (so to speak with the reader's indulgence) the persistent problem remained: how could the Book of Mormon hold theoretical superiority over the Bible, when the revelatory process had chosen a 17th century linguistic garment and vessel to compete with the New and the Old Testament? Pratt's writing which was, comparatively speaking, less "inspirational", did not become canonic, as Joseph Smith's and Brigham Young's had. Brigham Young did not really have to compete with his predecessor in office, nor with his prodigious rival, for he was shrewd enough to go along with the famous proverb: "let the cobbler stick to his last," in respect to avoid exploiting his position for the purpose of revelations. Brigham Young used the Bible as a storehouse illustrating his religious experience, whereas Pratt always scrutinized.[50] The wiser prophet communicated from experience, Pratt from his reverence for (faithful) truthfulness. In this vane he organized the Book of Mormon into chapters and verses, so that as of 1879, revelation could become subject to verifiable interpretation. This placed no less, but at the same time no more, than an indirect stamp on Mormon language development.

5.4.5 B. H. Roberts's and his Disciples' Language Defenses

Brigham Henry Roberts, (born 1857 in England, died 1933 in Salt Lake City), better known as B. H. Roberts, assembled in his hard-working life the basis of Mormon history. He understood "...

[50]T. Edgar Lyon, *Orson Pratt. Early Mormon Leader*. M. A. Thesis University of Chicago 1932; *The Essential Orson Pratt*. Foreword by David J. Whittaker in *Classics of Mormon Thought* (Salt Lake City, 1991). Pratt, in a sense, did for the Book of Mormon what Robert Estienne Stephanus (1503-1559) did for the Greek New Testament in 1551.

Mormonism as a religion and a social movement".[51] His original style was that of a formidable counter-puncher. He took on many a would-be Goliath in his *Defense of the Faith and the Saints*.[52] This loaded title for a "scrapbook" mirrors the double function of language, inasmuch as it is supposed to be a "tongue", "counseled in wisdom" by the "Lord".[53] The title in its royally sounding first part, "Defense of the Faith", takes up an ebullient line of positions for the defense. In its second part, "and the Saints" Roberts demonstrates a new people's religious behavior. He functioned in Mormonism as a kind of self-taught Horace Bushnell, and reused the Mormons' propensity for "radical heresy" as much as the Yale professor had a secret longing for a new un-dogmatic religious era.[54]

As a young man, Roberts had learned to write a sinewy editorial style at the Salt Lake Herald newspaper, before he left for missionary duty in England. I need not get into his subsequent election to the U.S. Congress, where he was denied his seat because of polygamy. All this can be read in his autobiography, prepared in the last year of his life.[55] In his most serious commitment to his church, he labored hard for thirty-six years (without a special honorarium, he noted), and plowed critically through the archival material in search of a comprehensive history of the LDS Church, which finally appeared in 1930 in definitive form in six volumes at the Deseret News Press.[56] Through all of his deeply religious service ran his common sense for the multiple forces that had shaped the Saints' movement, coupled

---

[51]Foreword by Sterling M. McMurrin, *The Autobiography of B. H. Roberts*, ed. Gary James Bergera (Salt Lake City, 1990), VIII.

[52]Appearing in the Deseret News Press, Salt Lake City, 1907.

[53]Alma 29:8.

[54]McMurrin, XIII-XIV and Barlow, 112.

[55]*The Essential B. H. Roberts*, ed. Brigham D. Madsen (Salt Lake City, 1999) [recte January 2000]. B. H. Roberts, *The Truth, The Way, The Life: An Elementary Treatise on Theology*, BYU Studies Monograph (Provo, 1994).

[56]*Comprehensive History of the Church of Jesus Christ of Latter-day Saints. Century 1.*

with a special feel of and for inspiration, and an earthy humor of the Lancasterian Englishman, whose accent he never gave up or could not overcome.

And yet the concerted work of several factors is illustrated as distinctly American, as if there was a parliament of religions at work. One such parliament was actually organized and assembled in 1893 at the World's Columbian Exhibition in Chicago. The LDS Church had not been invited to take its seat there. Roberts's defense was disallowed from the public arena, and so he acted like a shadow boxing champion defending a cause. If the other members of the Christian family thought that his church was a negligible sect, then the other denominations were, for the saintly defender,[57] "the great Christian sects". Subsequently he formulated in "scrapbook" entry form: "Mormonism – at that time he always placed the term in quotation marks – accepts and includes within its boundary-lines all truth. It is progressive and destined to become the religion of the age."[58] Relying on such a support system, he states that our faith-carrying language is meant "to perfect those who receive it".[59] In Roberts's opinion, the Book of Mormon can shoulder and remedy "defects of language", which "are found in it," "...especially in the first edition".[60] The problem of the charge of possible anachronisms in usage, such as New Testament quotes found in the Book of Mormon from pre-Christian times, does arise. Did Brigham Young and Orson Pratt clearly sense "the malleability of already canonized texts?"[61] Roberts came closer to Parley Pratt's adage: "What is

---

[57]*Defense*, 5 and 8.

[58]*Defense*, 21.

[59]*Defense*, 47.

[60]*Defense*, 260, written in 1905-06.

[61]Barlow, 95, referring to Brigham Young's *Journal of Discourses* 1: 117.

prophecy but history in reverse?"[62] Roberts tried to overcome this impasse by stressing that the Book of Mormon "verified the Bible". Thus, in sum, his biblical criticism was "profoundly ambivalent"[63] in Barlow's estimation.[64] Given his iron commitment to his work and the almost herculean work load, his responsibilities as the leading church historian of his time let him grow in stature. And yet we are sad to conclude, by modifying Barlow's summation, that B. H. Robert's selfmademanship had its shortcomings in respect to his linguistic prowess for his stewardship as a historian. He lacked linguistic preparation. His language command left him analytically somewhat unprepared and less original, although he stayed as uncompromisingly Mormon in his thought processes as Orson Pratt.[65] Thus I am not released from driving on in my task to find even more astute, but less dramatic models of language behavior on the part of the best Mormon minds. Still, generations of students were trained B. H. Roberts. His books persuaded the reader by their flamboyant style, about which his church superiors had reservations, and they curtailed his influence as best they could.

William Henry Chamberlin (1870-1921) was the first Mormon philosopher of religion and science. Trained in Chicago, California and at Harvard,[66] he was a superb classroom teacher at all three universities in the State of Utah, a man of insight and intelligence with a humble and democratic spirit,[67] who was much revered by his students. He taught the gamut: philosophy, religion, ancient languages, science, mathematics, geology, astronomy, psychology and

---

[62]*Voice of Warning*, chapter 2. In German "history in reverse" is skillfully translated by Carn into "eine Geschichte der Zukunft" (a history of the future).

[63]B. H. Roberts, *The Gospel* (Salt Lake City, 1888), 56ff.

[64]Barlow, 121-122.

[65]McMurrin, Foreword, *Autobiography*, VIII, XIV.

[66]Poor health, however, prevented him from finishing his Ph.D. degree in philosophy in 1917, after his resignation from BYU in the spring, 1916.

[67]Ralph V. Chamberlin, *Life and Philosophy of W. H. Chamberlin* (Salt Lake City, 1925), 216 (farewell address)..

education.[68] His command of language and languages old and new did not fall short by any standards; it may have even hurt him politically. Remember Hugo Grotius? The fact remains that Chamberlin must be considered the first Mormon university teacher, who applied modern methods of biblical criticism both in his publications and in his classes. According to his biographer, his brother Ralph, Chamberlin's philosophy could be termed "spiritual-pluralistic" which is based on a wide variety of reading in English and continental European literature.[69] Outstanding, in my opinion, is his linguistic insight that the power of the Mormon religion is not dependent on the ultimate truth or falsity of the forms and structures in which it is expressed. In keeping with this major progressive point, Chamberlin was never in favor with the leadership of the Church and consequently did not reach a high standing within it.

In Chamberlin's thinking within a scientific and linguistic context, God stoops, as it were, to the human level repeatedly to lift man up one more time, and in the process uses changing human ideas and expressions, even notions, the plausibility of which change over time.[70] Chamberlin, modest and reverent toward the convention of his religion, expressed, taught and emphasized "the provisional nature of revelation" and hence "the limitations of human language".[71] Men must accept new insights, new knowledge, and adjust their old faith accordingly, even in respect to essential tenets.[72] He was by no means a mere modern behaviorist who thought that communicating was just constructive work by itself. "O Zion! Dear Zion! Home of the free!" he exclaimed at BYU when he had returned to his beloved Utah, and

---

[68]See also Barlow, 129ff.

[69]W. L. Chamberlin, *Introduction to Philosophy: An Outline* (Salt Lake City, 1919), one of three books, published toward the end of his life. He left six fully expanded book manuscripts.

[70]*Life and Philosophy*,175-180. This is a pragmatic definition of truth after the philosophers Pearce and James.

[71]Barlow, 134.

[72]*Life and Philosophy*, 197.

remained without rancor over the reminiscences of an unhappy leaving the hilltop after his resignation from the faculty. His theory of knowledge climaxes, I think, in his theory of understanding the different modes of religious language. For Chamberlin "that idea is true which proves valid in the prolonged service of a human activity or purpose".[73] Mindful of his many brilliant formulations, I close with is own words: "There appears the possibility of the person's rising on an advanced plane, of his surviving a higher degree of individuality."[74] As an afterthought it must be stated that Chamberlin revolted with his teachings against the prevailing intellectualism of his time both in philosophy and in religion. For him and his approach in language, the spiritual element remained supreme, as it had been for Joseph Smith and Horace Bushnell as well. Perhaps his most linguistically succinct pronouncement was: "Unless we coexist with God, there was no ground for his living and growing."[75]

We learn from Mary Lythgoe Bradford's admirably written biography of Lowell Bennion (1908-1996)[76], a book, which earned the David W. & Beatrice C. Evans Annual Biography Award in 1995, that this academic teacher once sold a used Oldsmobile to his student Sterling McMurrin, now a famous scholar and erstwhile U.S. Commissioner for Education. It must have been a car of sterling quality, or else this fellow professor would never have called that the living legend, Lowel Bennion, the "Mormons' Saint".

Bennion was born to a distinguished Utah family in 1908. His father, Milton Bennion, was professor of philosophy and dean of education at the University of Utah. He was a prominent author of several books on the ethics in education. His wife Cora Lindsay also hailed from a prominent family. Milton Bennion had served as missionary in New

---

[73]Life, 344.

[74]Life, 378.

[75]Life, chapter 15 and 368.

[76]*Lowell L. Bennion: Teacher - Counselor - Humanitarian* (Salt Lake City, 1995).

Zealand. His son, who learned easily, was to become a missionary, and later, in 1928, mission president of the Swiss-German mission. Soon he could read, in the original German, Johann Wolfgang Goethe's works. At that time German graduate study was valued highly. So he studied philosophical sociology in Berlin, Vienna and Strasbourg. He did the philosophy research for his Ph.D. dissertation on Max Weber in German.[77] It must be noted that, for an American student, Max Weber's style is heavy and involved. Bennion wrote his dissertation in English but defended it in French.[78] His multi-linguistic brilliance made his final "landing" in Utah's ordinary English all the harder.

Although later in his career, Bennion could not pursue his studies of Max Weber and Emile Durkheim as theoretical sociological thinkers, he applied his youthful interim understanding of Weber to his sociological teaching method in his courses. When the re-discoverers of his dissertation maintain that Bennion's work applied "Weber's Calvinism-Capitalism" thesis to the development of Mormonism generally,[79] they are in error, for that is not the case. Of the three Weberian types of leaders only the charismatic type would fit Mormonism as it was inspired and founded by Joseph Smith. Unbeknown to Bennion, and to persons who later lauded him, nobody but Weber himself held a definite opinion in a couple of asides, which are not part of his main work Not treated in Bennion's dissertation, Weber's lesser known work bears the title "Die protestantischen Sekten und der Geist des Kapitalismus".[80] It

[77]*Max Weber's Methodology*. Les Presses Modernes (Paris, 1933).

[78]Eugene England, ed. (his former student at the University of Utah), *The Best of Lowell L. Bennion: Selected Writings 1928-1988* (Salt Lake City, 1988), chapter 6 "My Odyssey with Sociology", 44ff.

[79]Laurie Newman DiPadova and Ralph S. Brower, "A Piece of Lost History: Max Weber and Lowell L. Bennion," *The American Sociologist*, Fall 1992, vol. 23, No. 3, 37-51 and endnotes.

[80]*Frankfurter Zeitung*, Easter 1906. This newspaper article was then reprinted as "Kirche und Sekten" in: *Christliche Welt*, 1906, in 2 parts, 558ff. and 577ff.

appeared first as a major article which has almost book format, but never attracted the same attention as Weber's world-famous *Die protestantische Ethik und der Geist des Kapitalismus.*[81] For the posthumous editor of *Wirtschaft und Gesellschaft*[82] it was possible to know a letter, dated April 2, 1913, which Weber had written to the Tübingen professor of political economy, Robert Wilbrandt. Weber wrote there, that only a revealed religion, not science – as an exception to his typology – could decide value conflicts. Weber made it clear to his colleague Wilbrandt, that the scientific community of sociologists could not legitimately decide the authenticity of the Book of Mormon. And so the editor posthumously quoted Max Weber's final, positive judgment, meant as a compliment to the Mormon civilization: the achievements of the Mormons in the Salt Lake desert of Utah set at naught all rules of rational economy of new settlements.[83] This positive appraisal of the special conditions surrounding the social movement which developed into a Mormon civilization, placed it *outside* the typology proposed by Max Weber, with which Bennion dealt in his 1932/33 dissertation at Strasbourg. Bennion's language had to withhold a scientific vote for the absolute authenticity of the Book of Mormon.

Back home in Utah, Professor John A. Widtsoe[84] who was trained at Harvard and Göttingen, invited Bennion to open an Institute of Religion near the University of Utah. Dr. Bennion directed and taught at the helm of this institute for 26 years, ably assisted by his friend,

---

[81]Editions appeared in: "Gesammelte Aufsätze zur Kultursoziologie, II", *Jaffé`sches Archiv für Sozialwissenschaft*, vol. XX and XXI, 1904/05, in 1920, and photomechanically again in 1947: as well as posthumously in: *Wirtschaft und Gesellschaft*, 1976.

[82]Gesammelte Aufsätze, vol. I, 140; vol. II, 654, 696.

[83]Therefore it was only in 1976 that the various opinions from *Jaffésches Archiv für Sozialwissenschaft*, XX, 1904 and XXI, 1905, reached a final posthumous position via the photomechanical reprint of 1947. It did not yet mention the Mormons.

[84]See his outstanding work, *Joseph Smith: Seeker after Truth - Prophet of God* (Salt Lake City, 1951), 3rd collector`s ed. 1996.

Professor T. Edgar Lyon. Bennion did persuasive theoretical and practical work in the fields of the sociology of Mormon education, social and personal ethics, world and Mormon religion. His religious study manuals were in use for a life-time between 1930-1960 and even longer. Contrary to Chamberlin he was not trained in ancient languages, but he could point his finger at the litmus test for valuable as well as believable religious faith: "There can be no true spirituality without genuine social morality."[85] In other words, in religion he was more concerned with people believing than doctrine to be believed. That distinguished him from Elder Bruce R. McConkie.[86]

So Bennion's practical theological interest calls for hermeneutical standards, which continue Chamberlin's. If Barlow stresses Bennion's fondness for analogizing in "architectural guidelines",[87] it is also Bennion's gauge for functioning and ameliorated scriptural Mormon language. Here at last, it seems that our predilection for defining Mormon language as means of communicating among loyal participants in a Bennionesque fashion is scientifically *legitimate*. It is essentially a spiritually inspired language, functioning as means of communication. It does not receive an implicit value judgment, often alleged by church authorities, but a propositional clarity of a (Weberian) charismatic rule. Bennion does not want to read its meaning between the lines, but he wants you to read the lines just like the prophet Joseph Smith:[88] "Now if you had known this, you could have translated."[89] I did not know that until now. In my view this is the man-made or scaffolded grammar, consciously or unconsciously transporting man's language through language pitfalls and errors, which may become subject to correction on the part of the group. The group may take corrective action as well.

---

[85]*I believe* (Salt Lake City, 1983), VII.

[86]Barlow, 185-194.

[87]Barlow 200. Compare our "scaffold" simile 1.1 and 2.0 above.

[88]England, 334.

[89]Doctrine and Covenants 9:10.

Lowell Bennion's language correlated community considerations. In that sense Dr. Bennion, while he was still healthy, was a moralist with progressivist concerns, and not a conservative thinker such as his student Bruce R. McConkie, who related divinity considerations to church authority. For Professor Bennion, the human thought, even occasionally, surpasses the notion of suprahuman inspiration. Therefore, after so many decades of service and scholarship, his learned language has become that of a cultural standard for the Mormon community, and that constitutes a high degree of achievement in terms of discourse. His teaching manuals, written in brilliantly clear English, continued their influence indirectly even into the late nineteen eighties.

5.4.6 Rules of Order in the Language Usage of the Mormons

Coming closer to the final part of my investigation, I must clarify and check my description against the textual "reality" of the three main sources, the Book of Mormon, the Doctrine and Covenants, and perhaps the Pearl of Great Price. At this point I have hopes that I can still find a more descriptive criterion. There must be a terminological coherence in respect to my hypothesis, an examination of the Mormon language and its uses by outstanding Mormon teachers for the elite of Mormon college students for more than one generation.

In terms of descriptive linguistics I hope to have analyzed B. H. Robert's, William H. Chamberlin's, and Lowell L. Bennion's pragmatic contributions to the science of Mormon linguistics individually and to the pedagogy of the Mormon gospel. Am I entitled now to weigh them collectively as a *group* phenomenon? The ecclesiastical texts, quoted above by title, communicate with participants by way of an extended, action directed speaking style, as I presume to have recognized. The linguistic energy expanded in it is transferred through pedagogical channels which passed as religious energy through Joseph Smith's Doctrine and Covenants.

The motion of a Mormon "participant" is essentially the linguistic term for someone who is loyal to and steadfast in the collected rules of the canon, expressed in the Doctrine and Covenants and settled as former rules stored collectively. A new motion is called for and may be carried or not. Such motions are collectively "sustained", or if dependent indirectly on a revelation received, "ordained".[90] Occasionally the energy flow has to pass through a linguistic diaphragm as if temporarily stopped for a thinking period; witness Doctrine and Covenants 28:13: "For all things must be done in order, and by common consent in the church, by the prayer of faith."

Essentially then, while communication takes place, there are two streams of energy at work, one linguistic and one spiritual. These two flow and perhaps mix in the process of communication. The one arrives "top-down" through the channels of rules, as understood by explanations, the other "bottom-up" by collective testimony, undertaken for the purpose of mutual enlightenment; witness Doctrine and Covenants 8:11: "Ask ... that you may ... translate and receive knowledge from all those ancient records which have been hid up, that are sacred." These linguistic energies have "top-down" or predictive properties, as well as prescriptive "bottom-up" properties, making room for sermon, community service and other activities.

This overall ambiguity is very English, isn't it? It boils down to either "the ayes have it" or to "the nays carry the day". It is essentially a debate format, in terms of linguistics a highly regulated, sophisticated and ever fascinating one. The Saintly used Mormon language is probably in essence an orally inspired, debate-sharpened, ever changing **tongue**.

---

[90]Such as the one pertaining to the "elect lady" Emma Smith, "to expound scriptures, and to exhort the church", Doctrine and Covenants 25:7.

This notion of debate regulation, introduced by me, is crucial to understanding Mormon linguistics. Which chairperson has not loved to wade through the intricacies of Colonel Robert's Rules of Order, and tactically employ them? Seemingly authoritarian to the outsider – and which German does not start as a far-field outsider when coming to the United States? – this *debate manual* has some features in common with the Doctrine and Covenants. As *group* phenomenon the Covenant guarantees a say in the understanding of doctrine for the individual's covenant. The doctrines, on the other hand, seem shielded by the Covenant. The debating parliamentarian in the exercise of freedom of speech, or the listener remaining silent, are both protected. But also taken care is "... the freedom to unite in organizations for the achievement of common aims ... It has evolved ... into effective *group action*."[91]

If you are recognized by the chair, and have the floor, you may speak to the motion, unless ruled out of order. The rules of debate evolving into rules of order have centuries of parliamentary experience behind them, of many admirable and some crooked exercises. If you do not understand that someone else "has the floor", and fail to observe this crucial difference of "order", you are considered a person behaving out of order, which is much worse than tripping up in your convoluted grammar. Victor H. Yngve brilliantly drafted his germinal ideas – totally outside our context debated here, it is true[92] – on the basic linguistic foundation.[93] It is an eye-opener to check his rudimentary observations against the assembly regulations of the forerunner state, the so-called "Rules for the Conducting business in

[91]Alice Sturgis, *Standard code of parliamentary procedure*, 3rd ed. (New York, 1988), 2. Emphasis is mine.

[92]But he collegially gave me email permission to quote from and make use of it.

[93]"Building on the New Foundations: The Regulation of Debate" dated 4/22/98 in preliminary draft form, kindly sent to the author.

the House of Representatives of the Territory of Utah",[94] written shortly before that time by a committee for the general assembly of the State of Deseret. One hundred copies were published by authority of subsequent public printers. The adopted pamphlet contains twenty sections under five headings[95] on four pages. It tells the delegates representing the inhabitants of the territory what their duty is and what (not) to do. All of the main verbs used, call to parliamentary action: e.g. call to order, proceed to call ..., proceed to elect, compel ... attendance, preserve order, speak on points of order, decide questions of order, call ... to the chair, perform their duties, sit, allowed, constitute, order, shall govern, shall be called to order, ... shall always be in order, shall be postponed, shall be put first, ... shall have power to send. Nothing is visionary, or saintlike, everything is stated in terms of legal business. There is not a trace of Mormonism found in these parliamentary rules of the territory. And yet the revelations as rules for conducting Mormon "business" of the day, as well as the rules themselves applying these revelations in real Mormon life, go together as hand in glove. This is amazing. Mormons seem to use English both as a vehicle of faith and a vessel of order. Thus, faith is orderly, and order becomes a requisite of faith.

5.4.7 Summary of Investigative Results

The issue under consideration was to find the linguistically employed tools of the Mormons' language usage. This is particularly hard and risky if undertaken from an outsider's perspective. The debate format, embedded, but not quite hidden, is as contributory as the strait-jacket reference work of grammar as such. The "re-translated" language of the Book of Mormon is part 17th century King James Version English with the flavored syntax, as for example Doctrine and Covenants 29: 31 "For by the power of my Spirit created I them...,"

---

[94]Kept at the Western Americana (L. Tom Perry) Collection, Harold B. Lee Library, Vault Nr. 094 Ut 1 1854, and Vault 328. 79201 Ut 1 1852-59, courtesy of director Larry Draper and prof. emeritus Peter Crawley.

[95]Three of them rubricated under "Duty", two under "Order".

and a few interlaced 19th century American (burnt-over district) English expressions. The listening, or speaking, or writing group is just as involved as the individual participant. It attests to the enormous versatility of English. Mormon language usage is a faithful rendering of English.

The predictions of the scripture books do not refer exclusively to the real world outside[96] but to the spiritual "superworld" as well. For the short quote from Doctrine and Covenants 29:31 carries on and completes the thought in this very sense: "yea, all things both spiritual and temporal". The believer might be carried into that world by faith, greatly helped by astute linguistic behavior.[97]

The channeling between the participants top-down, as well as bottom-up, is synchronized by a well distributed energy flow, stored in the communal energy household: the Mormon religion. The procedures applied would have to be worked out in greater detail by other professional linguists at Brigham Young University, by both general linguists and scholars of the English Department together.[98] I

---

[96]Yngve, "Building on the New Foundation", section 4. 3, and explanatory personal email by Prof. Yngve to the author, dated 11 June, 1998.

[97]This point was made by Professor John W. Welch in an email communication to the author, dated 21 September, 1999.

[98]There is a very thorough and helpful material gathered in the 1973 and the 1974 *Conference of the Language of the Mormons. Language Research Center, Brigham Young University*, but it has since stopped from coming forth.

1973: John L. Sorensen, 1-5: Rachel L. Wallace, 6-19, with the "Working List of Mormon Language Lexicon," 10ff.; Vernon Lynn Tyler, "LDS International Glossary Guidelines,": Defined and Undefined Terms, 55-63, 58-62, "Possibly Difficult Terms", *63*.

1974: Gerrit de Jong, John L. Sorensen, and Vernon Lynn Tyler, 58ff., 73ff., 81ff.; Dallin Oaks et alii are preparing a book on the Mormon Names in the E. Mellen Press, New.York for 2001, in which a promising article on the names of Latter-day Saint History by Eric A. Eliason will appear. See also John W. Van Cott

may have been able to perceive the *modus operandi* in some general terms at this time. Further research would have to be mindful of primary spiritual norms underlying team translation of early Mormon faith material, particularly in respect to grammatical correctness, considered important, but ultimately of secondary significance.

Authoritative personalities speaking astutely, such as Brigham Young or Joseph Fielding Smith, have perpetuated and guaranteed the functioning of the community. But still, their language too is based on debatable patterns and thrives on parliamentary procedures. The linguistic orbit of Mormonism is coherent but flowing, deliberate and intelligent. Both the presiding office, represented by President Gordon B. Hinckley, and the average Mormon Saint play their role inside, which is counted and assessed. Both energy flows ultimately meet and amalgamate in verbal religious images. God's icons producing mill grinds slowly,[99] neither too soon nor too late in the latter-day.

A unity of knowhow achieves common aims which in their diversity have to be within linguistic reach. In an admirable, but nevertheless slightly ironic sense, the language usage of the Mormons is in order, as long as it continues debates among loyal participants, allowing the outsider to knock ever so gently at the door marked **Christian language**.

5.5 Latter-day Self-Control in Checking the Christian Language Order

There seems to exist a peculiar system of checking and balancing fulfilment and order within Mormon English language usage.

---

and Kimball T. Harper, *Utah Place Names: A Comprehensive Guide to the Origin of Geographic Names* (Salt Lake City, 1990).

[99]See the task hierarchies drawn by Victor Yngve in "Rules of Order", *LACUS FORUM*, XXV, Aug. 1998, 6-7 and 9.

Sometimes it is facetiously called "Mormonspeak", which might be the gradation, if any, between it and normal English on a scale. A dialogue is kept open with the "larger stream" of English secular "thought and with human experience as a whole".[100] There seems room for registering efforts not to widen a possible language gap on either side. But between "agency" and deliberate order there still is some opening. It may have something to do with more self-control and other difficulties that call for some explaining.

An apt example would be the keeping of the addition in the Church's name, "Latter-day Saints" in the extended name of the young Church in 1834: "The Church of Jesus Christ of Latter-day Saints".One might have expected, after Sidney Rigdon's excommunication took place in 1844, that the ex-spokesman's suggestion would have been rescinded. Not so. It was a motion, made by Rigdon, seconded by Newel K. Whitney, while President Joseph Smith was chosen moderator, after remarks by the members, which was passed and carried unanimously.[101] The churches abroad and the newspaper were notified. The innovation was announced by the spokesman himself the following Sunday, "that the Prophet and the high council had agreed to his suggestion to change the name of the church from 'The Church of Christ' to 'The Church of the Latter-day Saints'," emphasizing the assumed proximity of the millennium.[102] The re-naming betrays a high degree of flexibility.

A counter-example of the self-control of the language order would be the following: the Doctrine and Covenants are nowadays issued as

---

[100]Cf. the engaging intellectual journal *The Dialogue: A Journal of Mormon Thought,* edited by Neal and Rebecca Chandler.

[101]*History of the Church of Jesus Christ of Latter-day Saints*, vol. II, ed. B. H. Roberts (Salt Lake City, 1965), 62.

[102]Richard S. Van Wagoner, *Sidney Rigdon: A Portrait of Religious Excess* (Salt Lake City, 1994), 149. This is not to overlook the prophet`s revelation of 1838 to finalize the name of the church in its present title (re-addition of "of Jesus Christ").

"Containing Revelations Given to Joseph Smith, the Prophet", and are published by the Church in Salt Lake City. But the Doctrine and Covenants were originally issued as "Carefully selected from the Revelations of God and compiled by Joseph Smith. Oliver Cowdery. Sidney Rigdon. Frederick G. Williams (Presiding Elders of the said Church) Proprietors. Kirtland, Ohio Printed by F. G. Williams & Co for the Proprietors 1835." It is clear why after the excommunications of Rigdon and Cowdery they had to stay unmentioned. In keeping with that self-control, Doctrine and Covenant 8:6-7 attributes "the gift of Aaron" to Oliver Cowdery, where the original Book of Commandments 7:3 had admitted to his "[the] gift of working with the rod."[103] Embarrassing usage had to be rescinded.

Earlier in this book I have corroborated that the Mormon religion is a Christian religion rather than a sect. Now I have to speculate a little bit more on the ecclesiastical history of that notion. As Christianity grew outside the Roman legal system -- NB "*religio*" is not a Roman legal category --, so did Mormon Christianity outside the American legal system at least until 1854, when the early territorial rules were published. The temples which are owned by the LDS Church, are indirectly owned or at least dedicated to Jesus Christ. During the rise and development of Early Christianity, God, Christ and the Catholic saints became immortals in the medieval ecclesiastical legal sense. A remarkable distinction separated Catholic saints from ordinary mortals, who legally deceased upon their death: they, the old saints, "lived" on, because the Catholic Church wanted it that way. Thus the traditional saints need not rise again during the latter-days, for they have already inherited their place in heaven.[104] Since the LDS

[103]Larry E. Morris, "Oliver Cowdery`s Vermont Years," *BYU Studies*, vol. 39,1 2000, 106-129.

[104]Heinz Holzhauer, "Unsterblichkeit und Recht,"*Beiträge zur Rechtsgeschichte*, ed. Stefan C. Saar/Andreas Roth (Berlin, 2000), 57.

"sainthood" stands only for the membership status in their church,[105] it follows that members lose their ecclesiastic legal status as a person upon their death, just as any other American citizen. Now the entitlement of the LDS Church as corporation under public law – begging the reader's indulgence for a Germanic sounding comparative legal explanation[106] – was prefigured in the *person* of Christ.[107] The language use is selective.

The acceptance of the Territory of Utah into U.S. statehood within the United States in 1896 has presupposed a secularization of commercial church corporations, which amounted to a self-control, negotiated in plain American English with the federal government in Washington, D. C.: for *lex posterior derogat legi priori*: a subsequently promulgated statute rescinds prior law. That legally promulgated separation of church and state had been put on its head in part by Joseph Smith's King Follet Funeral Oration, redefining "the rising into heaven" thus: "God that sits enthroned is a man like one of yourselves;" the prophet, as a corollary, presupposed "a once-mortal God".[108] And if man's mind, "the intelligent part is coequal with God himself,"[109] then the rising of man's spiritual remains to Him, is an entirely different undertaking. It sharply separates the resurrection process from that defined by traditional Christianity: the responsibility for its successfully taking place is here partially loaded on the shoulders of the living, in that they have to help rise the dead "to be made perfect".[110] Hence, according to Mormon theology, "God

---

[105]James K. Lyon, entry "Saints", *Encyclopedia of Mormonism*, ed. by Daniel L. Ludlow, vol. 3, 1249f. It is interesting to note that Rigdon`s original thinking is not questioned any more.

[106]Under German law, churches are constructed as "juridical persons": *Körperschaften des öffentlichen Rechts.*

[107]H. Holzhauer, 58.

[108]King Follet Funerary Oration, 7 April 1844, William Clayton Report Version, compiled and edited by Andrew F. Ehat and Lyndon W. Cook, *The Words of Joseph Smith* (Orem, 1994), 357 and editors` endnotes on 399.

[109]Ehat 359.

[110]Ehat 360; Hebrews 11: 40.

himself should come down among the children of men ...that he should bring to pass the resurrection of the dead, ...".[111] This last, quite important example, channels the self-control of the Christian language order at the same time down to earth and back into orbit. What a surge that must be when the latter-day comes. If it needs to be, the Mormon language usage is predictive.

A less striking, but nevertheless relevant example of the self-control in respect to the Mormon, and at the same time Christian, language order is the motto chosen by the Council of Fifty, when it authorized "general" Joseph Smith from Nauvoo, Illinois, to run for president of the United States in 1844. Sidney Rigdon from Pennsylvania was chosen as his third place vice-presidential running mate. Their political campaign flyer pictured a rock[112] from which sun rays hit the waves of an ocean. Amazingly three barely visible Latin terms, "*error*," "*vis*," and "*veritas*", on the picture are standing for their platform! The motto means: "the shining light's power will change human uncertainty into truthfulness". It is clearly a religiously inspired metaphor, although one betraying the handwriting of yet another "seasoned if erratic" newspaper editor, W. W. Phelps.[113] The voters were to be convinced that these two Mormon "Reform Party" candidates were representing "a viable political force". Here church Latin and its historical tradition, which was taken over and changed by English political language usage a long time ago, shows self-control and Christian inspired language order of the old kind (in Latin!) for the purpose of acceptance by the public. If need be, a

[111]Mosiah 13:34-35.

[112]Quoting in capital-lettered Latin, "SUPER HANC PETRAM AEDIFICABO", part of Matthew 16:18 [omitting "my community"] (courtesy Utah State Historical Society).

[113] See Wagoner, *Sidney Rigdon*, 331. Apparantly it was used also in Rigdon`s own sermon of April 7, 1844, alluding to a kingdom of heaven turned into true government, Wagoner 333. See also Joseph Smith, *General Smith`s Views of the Powers and Policy of the Government of the United States* (Nauvoo, 1844), 12.

motto may even be expressed in Latin in order to assure political success.

The following is a final attempt to describe an important, controlled language change. The posthumously appearing Pearl of Great Price, published in England in 1851, after it had been declared canonical, it was found to contain revelations, doubling some of the ones revealed before in the Doctrine and Covenants. These sections were taken from the Pearl of Great Price by the General Conference on the basis of an unanimous vote, and in this cleansed form sustained as holy scripture in 1902.[114] Clarity overrules the historical context.

An important point of contact-in-order between the King James Version English of the Book of Mormon and everyday English is this: The narration tries to persuade the believer in terms of "... everyday struggles of their people[.] ... as expression ... of their understanding of God and his will[.]... establishing peace based on righteous principles."[115] Both the traditional Testaments of the Bible and the Book of Mormon teach righteous principles. In the Old Testament and the Book of Mormon the concept of original sin is not part of the principles of righteousness. In 2 Nephi 2:25 the "righteous" enjoyment of life is tied to Adam's "fortunate" beginning of morality.[116] "Joy is a by-product of righteous, self-fulfilling living as Jesus indicated in the Beatitudes."[117] So, in a sense, the two guidelines for Christian living, the Bible and the Book of Mormon, are as two spiritual bonds in a relation of typological checks and balances to

---

[114]Lowel L. Bennion, *Einführung ins Evangelium*; translated from the English by Max Zimmer, 2nd ed.

[115]Lowell L. Bennion. *The Book of Mormon. A Guide to Christian Living* (Salt Lake City 1985), 5-6.

[116]See 2 Nephi 2:25 and R. W. B. Lewis, *The American Adam: Innocence, Tragedy, and Tradition in the Nineteenth Century* (Chicago, 1955), 54-73, 71-72.

[117]Lowell L. Bennion, *The Book of Mormon. A Guide to Christian Living*, 51.

each other. Both invoke obedience to the commands and the doctrines which these two reservoirs of religious strength demand separately from their Christian believers. The Holy Bible, in 1979, was cross-referenced to the standard works of the Church of Jesus Christ of Latter-day Saints, and one day a critical edition of the Book of Mormon,[118] cross-referenced to the two Testaments of the Bible, will also appear. Neither the church hierarchy nor the rank-and-file has anything to fear but fear itself[119] of critically[120] glossed revelations. This self-scrutinizing labor of appreciating the common spiritual heritage will rigorously reaffirm the genuine Christian language order. As Joseph Smith, the prophet, is dependent on Jesus Christ, the savior, so the Book of Mormon is co-founded on the Old and the New Testament. With due respect, the Book of Mormon in a wider sense also reveals the latter-day self-control of the Christian language usage. Now it has become clear why one can approach the essential nucleus of the Book of Mormon from several venues, including the broad avenue of linguistics.

Whether the approaches start from Christian writer's analogues, or ultimately patristic traditions' views, the authenticity of the Book of Mormon, the rule of Christian language order, or the self-control function of the Mormon language usage, they all radially point to the

---

[118]Undertaken by Prof. Royal Skousen et aliis in *Book of Mormon Critical Text of FARMS Critical Text Project*, vols. I-III, until letter M (c) 1984, 1986, 1987. For gaining a historical perspective see Benjamin Winchester, *Synopsis of the Holy Scriptures and Concordance* ... VIII plus 256 pp. (Philadelphia, 1842).

[119]This famous adage actually was coined by Hugo Grotius, while he was seventeen and a half years old, in his first celestial drama, *Adamus Exul* (The Hague, 1601), v. 1426; see above, Chapter 3, f.n. 106. It helps to have knowledgeable speech writers.

[120]John W. Welch, "Introduction to the Book of Mormon Critical Text," *Deseret Language and Linguistic Society*. Fourteenth Annual Symposium. Provo, Utah, 17-18 March, 1988, 1-7. Prof. Jack Welch's assistant, Jedford Woodworth, emailed that Welch is in the process of editing Joseph Smith's Book of Mormon dictation manuscripts critically in 8 volumes.

center, which is constitutionally and spiritually governing *and* governed at the same time.

Arrived as free agent, equipped with a felicity of mind at the threshold of Mormondom, we have nothing to fear but fear of commitment itself.

6. Selected Bibliography

6.1 Primary Literature

D'Anghiera, Pietro Martyr. *De rebus oceanis et orbe novo decades octo*. Paris: 1533.

DAS BUCH MORMON Ein weiterer Zeuge für Jesus Christus. Frankfurt am Main, Kirche Jesu Christi der Heiligen der Letzten Tage, 1995.

De Laet, Joannes. *Origine in Notae ad dissertationem Hugonis Grotii*. Amsterdam: Elzevier's 1643.

DIE KÖSTLICHE PERLE. Frankfurt am Main: Kirche Jesu Christi der Heiligen der Letzten Tage, 1995.

Ehat, Andrew F. & Cook, Lyndon W., compiled and edited with a Foreword by Truman G. Madsen. *The Words of Joseph Smith*. The contemporary accounts of the Nauvoo discourses of the Prophet Joseph. Provo: Brigham Young University, 1980. Third Printing Grandin Book Company 1994.

Hugo Grotius. *Bewijs van de waere Godsdienst*. Sine loco 1622; 7 more Dutch eds. until the end of the 18th century; 3 German eds. during the 17th century; no English translation.

—. *De Veritate Religionis Christianae*. Leiden: 1627; first anonymous trl. into English London 1632, 5 more English eds in the 17th, 17 more Engl. eds in the 18th century, and 9 more until 1829.

—. *Defensio fidei catholicae de Satisfactione Christi adversus Faustum Socinum Senensem*. Leiden: 1617; Engl. trl. by W. H. *A Defence of the Catholick Faith Concerning the Satisfaction of Christ*, see Termeulen-Diermanse, Bibliographie, Nr. 932.

—. *Sacra in qvibus Adamvs Exvl traegoedia*. The Hague: 1601; Engl. trl. Francis Barham: *Adams Exile or The prototype of Paradise Lost*. London: 1839.

—. *Tragoedia Christus Patiens*. Leiden: 1608; Engl. trl. by John Legatt. *Christs passion. A tragedie*. London: 1640.

—. *Dissertatio de Origine Gentium.*

Americanarum. Paris (?): 1642; Engl. trl. Edmund Goldsmid. Bibliotheca Curiosa. Privately printed Edinborough 1884.

Jessee, Dean J., ed. *The Papers of Joseph Smith*. 2 vols. Salt Lake City: Deseret Book Company, vol. i 1989; vol. ii 1992.

LEHRE UND BÜNDNISSE der Kirche Jesu Christi der Heiligen der Letzten Tage. Frankfurt am Main: Kirche Jesu Christi der Heiligen der Letzten Tage, 1995.

P. W. = Penn, William. *URIM AND THUMMIM or the Apostolical Doctrines of LIGHT AND PERFECTION MAINTAINED*. Printed [*sine loco*] in the Year 1674.

Skousen, Royal, ed. et alii. *Book of Mormon Critical Text of FARMS Critical Text Project,* vols. I-III, until letter M (c) 1984, 1986, 1987.

Smith, Joseph: *General Smith's Views of the Powers and Policy of the Government of the United States*. Nauvoo: John Taylor Printer 1844.

Spencer, John. *De Urim et Thummim*. Cambridge, England: 1670.

THE BOOK OF MORMON Another Testament of Jesus Christ. Salt Lake City: The Church of Jesus Christ of Latter-day Saints, 1998.

THE DOCTRINE AND COVENANTS of the Church of Jesus Christ of Latter-day Saints. Salt Lake City: The Church of Jesus Christ of Latter-day Saints, 1998.

THE HOLY BIBLE containing the OLD AND NEW TESTAMENTS. Authorized King James Version. With Explanatory Notes and Cross References to the Standard Works of The Church of Jesus Christ of Latter-day Saints. Salt Lake City, Utah: The Church of Jesus Christ of Latter-day Saints, 1995.

THE PEARL OF GREAT PRICE. Salt Lake City: The Church of Jesus Christ of Latter-day Saints, 1998.

6.2 Auxiliaries (Encyclopedia, Dictionaries, Guides to Sources)

Bitton, Davis, ed. *Historical Dictionary of Mormonism*. Metuchen & London: 1994.

Cross, F. L. and Livingstone, E. A., eds. *The Oxford Dictionary of the Christian Church*. Third edition. Oxford: University Press, 1997, 1115-16.

Eggenberger, Oswald. "*Mormonen,*" *Religion in Geschichte und Gegenwart*. 3. Auflage, IV. Band. Tübingen: 1960, Spalte 1138-1141.

Ludlow, Daniel H., ed. *Encyclopedia of Mormonism*. iv vols. New York: Macmillan Co., 1992. Selected edition 1995.

McConkie, Bruce R. *Mormon Doctrine*. iv volumes. Salt Lake City, 1966. Translated by Hans-Wilhelm Kelling. *Mormon Doctrine. Deutschsprachige Ausgabe*. Bad Reichenhall: LDS Books Schubert & Roth, 1991/1992.

Termeulen, Jacob / Diermanse, P. J. J. *Bibliographie des écrits imprimées de Hugo Grotius*. The Hague: Martinus Nijhoff, 1950.

Whittaker, David J. *Mormon Americana. A guide to Sources and Collections in the United States*. Provo: BYU Studies, 1995.

6.3 Concordances

Gellinek, Christian. *Hugo Grotius Drama Concordance*. Columbus: Camden House, 1983.

Madsen, Truman G. *The Concordance of the Doctrinal Statements of Joseph Smith*. Salt Lake City: 1985.

Ricks, Eldin. *Thorough Concordance of the LDS Standard Works*. Provo: F A R M S, 1995.

Shapiro, R. Gary, compiled. *An Exhaustive Concordance of the Book of Mormon, the Doctrine and Covenants and the*

Pearl of Great Price. Salt Lake City: G. P. Hawkes Publ. Inc., 1977.

Winchester, Benjamin. *Synopsis of the Holy Scriptures and Concordance ...* VIII. Philadelphia: 1842.

6.4 Periodicals

BYU Studies. A Multidisciplinary Latter-day Saint Journal. Editor in chief: John W. Welch. Provo: Brigham Young University.

Dialogue. A Journal of Mormon Thought. Editors Neal and Rebecca Chandler. Shaker Heights, OH.

F A R M S: Foundation for Ancient Research and Mormon Studies. Director Daniel Peterson. Provo, Utah.

Sunstone. Salt Lake City, Utah.

The Ensign of the Church of Jesus Christ of Latter-day Saints, ed. Marlin K. Jensen. Salt Lake City, Utah.

6.5 Secondary Literature

Alexander, Thomas G. *Mormonism in Transition 1880-1930. A History of the Latter-Day Saints*. Urbana: University of Illinois Press, 1987.

—. "The Reconstruction of Mormon Doctrine", *Sunstone: Mormon Experience, Scholarship, Issues and Art,* vol. 22:3-4. Issue 115-116, June 1999, 15-28.

Arrington, Leonard J. *Great Basin Kingdom: An Economic History of the Latter-Day Saints 1830-1900*. Lincoln, Nebraska: 1958; Rp 1966.

—. *Brigham Young. American Moses*. University of Illinois: 1986.

—. ed. *The Presidents of the Church*. Salt Lake City, 1986 / 1993.

—. Bitton, Davis. *The Mormon Experience. A History of the LDS*. New York: Alfred A. Knopf, 1979; second ed. 1992.

Backman Jr., Milton V. *Joseph Smith's First Vision*. Salt Lake City: 1971.

Barlow, Philip L. *Mormons and the Bible*. Oxford University Press: 1991.

Bennion, Lowell L. *The Book of Mormon. A Guide to Christian Living*. Salt Lake City: Deseret Book Company, 1985.

Bitton, Davis and Arrington, Leonard J. *The Mormons and their Historians*. Salt Lake City: University of Utah Press, 1988.

—. Beecher, Maureen U., ed. *New Views of Mormon History. A Collection of Essays in Honor of Leonard J. Arrington*. 1997.

Benz, Ernst. "Der Mensch als Imago Dei," (1971). Rp in: *Urbild und Abbild. Der Mensch und die mythische Welt*. Leiden: Brill, 1974, 475-508.

—. *Der Heilige Geist in Amerika*. Düsseldorf: Diederichs, 1970.

Brodie, Fawn M. *No Man Knows my History. The Life of Joseph Smith*. Second edition. New York: Alfred A. Knopf, 1986.

Brooke, John L. *The Refiner's Fire. The Making of Mormon Cosmology 1644 - 1844*. Cambridge University Press, 1994.

Bushman, Richard L. *Joseph Smith and the Beginnings of Mormonism*. University of Illinois Press, 1988.

—. *Making Space for the Mormons: Ideas of Sacred Geography in Joseph Smith's America. Leonard J. Arrington Lecture Series* Nr. 2. Logan:1997.

Bushnell, Horace. *God in Christ. Three discourses ... with a preliminary Dissertation on Language (1848)*. Hartford, 1849. Rp New York: AMS Press, 1972.

Cheney, Mary M. *Collected Works of Horace Bushnell*. 11 vols. plus 1 vol. 1876 -1881. Second edition. New York: 1903.

Easton Black, Susan and Tate, Jr., Charles D. *Joseph Smith. The Prophet, The Man*. BYU. Provo: 1993.

Friedrich, Hans-Martin. *Die gefälschte Offenbarung*. Basel: Brunnenfokus, 1997 (recte 1998).

Furniss, Norman F. *The Mormon Conflict 1850-1859.* Yale University Press, 1960.

Gellinek, C. *Elementare Linguistik. Grundzüge der Sprachwissenschaft*. Berne: 1980

—. "Die Verteidigung der Wahrheit der christlichen Religion ...", *Festschrift für Arval L. Streadbeck*, ed. by Wolff von Schmidt, Gerhard Knapp and Heinz F. Rahde. Berne: 1981, 53-64.

—. *Hugo Grotius*. Twayne World Authors Series. TWAS 680. Boston: 1983.

—. "The Principal Literary Analogues of John Milton's Paradise Lost," *A Festschrift in Honor of Ernst S. Dick*. ed. by Winder McConell. Göppingen: 1989, 77-82.

—. *Christus in Amerika? Mormonentum als christliche Religion in vergleichender Kirchengeschichte*. Münster: Agenda Verlag, 1999.

Hansen, Klaus J. *Mormonism and the American Experience*. University of Chicago Press: w. y. 1981.

Hauth, Rüdiger. *Tempelkult und Totentaufe*. Gütersloh: GTB Sachbuch, 1985. Reworked Diss. masch. Aarhus, Denmark: Der Mormonentempel und seine Rituale 1986.

—. "Mormonen," *Evangelisches Kirchenlexikon*. Dritte Auflage, III, L-R. Göttingen: 1992, Spalten 547-549.

—. *Die Mormonen. Glaubensreligion oder Christliche Kirche?*. Freiburg: Herderbücherei, 1995. Second edition.

Hill, Donna. *Joseph Smith. The First Mormon*. New York: Knopf, 1979.

Introvigne, Massimo. *Les Mormons. Fils d'Abraham*. Belgium: Edition Brepols, 1991.

Leone, Mark P. *The Roots of Modern Mormonism*. Harvard University Press, 1979.

Meinhold, Peter. "Die Anfänge des amerikanischen Geschichtsbewußtseins," *Saeculum,* 5. 1954. Freiburg / München: 1954, 65-85.

Meyer, Eduard. *Ursprung und Geschichte der Mormonen*. Halle: 1912. Translated into English by Heinz F. Rahde and Eugene Seaich. Salt Lake City: 1961. Rp. Hildesheim /New York: Olms, 1970.

Mössmer, Albert. *Die Mormonen. Die Heiligen der Letzten Tage*. Solothurn:Walter Verlag, 1995.

Mullen, Robert. *Die Mormonen: Geschichte einer Glaubensbewegung*. Weilheim: O. W. Barth Verlag, 1966. (1968 translation of the American title from 1966)

Nibley, Hugh. *An Approach to the Book of Mormon*. Third edition. Salt Lake City, 1988.

—. *The World and the Prophets*. Ed. by John W. Welch et alii. Salt Lake City, 1987.

O'Dea, Thomas F. *Sociology and the Study of Religion 1957 / 1964*. New York and London: Basic Books, 1970.

Olshausen, Theodor. *Geschichte der Mormonen oder Jüngsten-Tages-Heiligen in Nordamerika*. Göttingen: Vandenhoeck und Ruprecht, 1856.

Packer, Boyd K. *Der Heilige Tempel*. Frankfurt am Main: 1984. (American original edition Salt Lake City: 1980)

Pratt, Parley P. *The Voice of Warning*. Originally 1838; British edition 1841; German translation: *Die Stimme der Warnung*. Rp. 1901.

Prince, Gregory A. *Power from on High. The Development of the Mormon Priesthood*. Salt Lake City: Signature Books, 1995.

Quinn, D. Michael, ed. *The New Mormon History. Revisionist Essays on the Past*. Salt Lake City: Signature Books, 1992.

Reps, John W. *The Making of Urban America. A History of City Planning in the United States*. Princeton University Press: 1965.

—. *Cities of the American West. A History of Frontier Urban Planning*. Princeton University Press, 1992. Third printing.

Roberts, Brigham H. *Defense of the Faith and the Saints*. 2 vols. Salt Lake City, 1907.

—. *Comprehensive History of the Church of Jesus Christ of Latter-day-Saints*. 6 vols. Salt Lake City: Deseret News, 1930. Seventh volume Salt Lake City: 1932. Second edition 1946ff.; Rp. third ed. Provo: Brigham Young University, 1965; fourth ed. 1980.

Rogerson, John W. *W. M. L. de Wette. Founder of Modern Biblical Criticism. An International Biography*. Sheffield: JSOT Press, 1992.

Scharffs, Gilbert. *Mormonism in Germany. A History of the Church of Jesus Christ of Latter-day Saints in Germany between 1840 and 1970.* Salt Lake City: Deseret Book Company, 1970.

Shipps, Jan. *Mormonism. The Story of a New Religious Tradition*. University of Illinois: 1985.

Smith, Donna. *Joseph Smith: The First Mormon*. Doubleday: 1977.

Stark, Rodney. *The Rise of Christianity*. San Francisco: Harper Collins and Harper, 1997.

Taylor, P. A. M. *Expectations Westward: The Mormon and the Emigration of the British Converts in the Nineteenth Century*. Cornell University Press: 1966.

Tobler, Douglas F. and Wadsworth, Nelson. *Der Weg zum Licht: Die Geschichte der Mormonen in Bildern und Texten*. Kehl am Rhein: Swan, 1987 (American original edition: *The History of the Mormons in Photography and Texts*. St. Martin's Press: 1987).

Van Baaren, J. I. *Mormonen en hun leer in het licht van de bijbel.* Amsterdam: Stichting Moria 1986.

Van Biema, David. "Kingdom Come," TIME MAGAZINE, August 4, 1997

Van der Valk, M. H. A. *Zur Beurteilung des Propheten der Mormonen Joseph Smith jun*. 1921. Translated from the Dutch by A. Basedow. Leipzig: 1923.

Van Orden, Bruce. *Building Zion. The Latter-day Saints in Europe*. Salt Lake City: Deseret Book Company, 1996.

Van Pelt, J. R., ed. "Mormonen," *Realenzyclopädie für protestantische Theologie und Kirche*. XIII. Band. Leipzig: 1903, 465-78.

Van Wagoner, Richard S. *Sidney Rigdon. A Portrait of Religious Excess*. Salt Lake City: Signature Books, 1994.

Welch, John W., ed. *Reexploring the Book of Mormon*. The FARMS Updates. Salt Lake City: Deseret Book Company, 1992.

—, ed. *The Truth, The Way, The Life. Elementary Treatise on Theology by B. H. Roberts* (posthumous 1933). Second edition Brigham Young University Studies: 1996.

Werner, Morris R. *Brigham Young*. New York: 1925. German translation with the added subtitle 'Der Moses der Mormonen'. Zürich and Leipzig: 1928. English Rp. Westport: 1975.

7. Biographical Note

Professor emeritus **Christian Gellinek** worked at the Institute of Social and Economic Research, University of Newfoundland, St. John's, Canada, 1995-96, at the Institut für vergleichende Städtegeschichte at Münster University in Germany, 1987-95, and at the University of Florida, Gainesville, USA, 1971-87.

He was formerly a student of civil and ecclesiastical law at the University of Göttingen, Germany (Rudolf Smend), a Latin instructor at Pickering College, Newmarket, Ontario (Canada's oldest Quaker school), and a junior faculty member at Yale University 1963-71.

He received his Ph.D. from the Yale German Department in 1964, his "Habilitation"(Dr. phil.-habil.) from Basel University, Switzerland. He started his career with an article on "Daniel's Vision of Four Beasts", published in *Germanic Review* 1966. After an extended Fulbright research stay at the Peace Palace in The Hague, The Netherlands, Twayne published his biography on Hugo Grotius, Boston 1983.

Gellinek was visiting professor in various disciplines at Basel, Poznan, Poland, Salt Lake City and Provo, Utah, at UCLA, California, and at Münster in Westphalia, where he carried out urban, peace and migration research. He is married to Josepha Gellinek-Schellekens, and they have four children.

Born in Mecklenburg and raised in Bremen, Germany, Professor **Hans-Wilhelm Kelling** served a mission for the Church of Jesus Christ of Latter-day Saints in the eastern United States from 1953 to 1955. He received a B. A. degree from Brigham Young University in 1958 and attended Stanford University from 1958 to 1962 on a Woodrow Wilson Fellowship. At Stanford he received both his M. A. and Ph.D. degrees in German and French literature and philosophy. He did the research for his dissertation at the University of Göttingen.

From 1973 to 1976 Prof. Kelling served as mission president in the Germany Munich Mission. At Brigham Young University he is a professor of German Literature and Cultural History, Director of the European Studies and the European Internship Programs. He has directed study abroad programs in Salzburg and Vienna and published books and articles on Goethe and other subjects. His noted *Deutsche Kulturgeschichte* was used by Prof. Gellinek at the University of Florida with enthusiasm. Kelling is married to Joyce Kay Coy Kelling, and they have four children.